ARIZONA CATTLEWOMAN

The Remarkable Life of Carrie Swigart Fraizer

Betty Barr

BrockingJ Books   Sonoita, Arizona

Copyright © 2017 by Betty Barr

All rights reserved. No part of this book may be reproduced or transmitted in any form or by any means, electronic or mechanical, including photocopying, recording, or by any information storage and retrieval system, without permission in writing from the author.

To contact the author or order
additional copies of this book
write to us at:
P.O. Box 226
Sonoita, Arizona 85637
www.BrockingJbooks.com

This edition was prepared for publication by
Ghost River Images
5350 East Fourth Street
Tucson, Arizona 85711
www.ghostriverimages.com

On the Cover: Carrie Swigart and her sister, Rhoda claimed adjoining homesteads. Carrie is seen looking out the window of the first structure erected on her side of the line. Rhoda is at the doorway in the snow. Late 1913.

On the Back Cover: Jim and Carrie Swigart Fraizer with their son, Samuel, in front of the house they built on Jim Fraizer's homestead which adjoined Carrie's parcel. 1920.

ISBN: 978-0-9790261-5-7

Library of Congress Control Number: 2017906148

Printed in the United States of America

September, 2017

Dedicated to Janet Rowley Thompson

Contents

Acknowledgements 9
Foreword 11

Chapter One - The Journey West 15
Chapter Two - Staking the Claim 21
Chapter Three - Single Women 25
Chapter Four - Necessities of Life 29
Chapter Five - Proving Up 35
Chapter Six - Visitors From Home 41
Chapter Seven - Romance on the Range 51
Chapter Eight - Making a Home 59
Chapter Nine - Starting a Family 65
Chapter Ten - Community Spirit 75
Chapter Eleven - Alone Again 95
Chapter Twelve - The Legacy Endures 107

Bibliography 115
Index 119
About the Author 129

Acknowledgements

Tim Capron, whose wife, Rhonda is a distant cousin on the Swigart side of Carrie Fraizer's family, was the first to suggest a book on her life. A new resident of Arizona, Tim read a few articles about this remarkable woman and then traveled to Sonoita to see first-hand where she had homesteaded. He and Rhonda stopped at the Sonoita Elgin Fire Department to ask for help with some historical background, and were told to contact me. The rest is history, no pun intended.

Carrie's grandchildren, Jim Rowley, Janet Rowley Thompson, and Lynn Fraizer Kelley generously shared memories of their grandmother, along with photos, and news clippings which were invaluable in helping to piece together Carrie's amazing life. Janet went above and beyond what I ever dared to expect, spending countless hours transcribing oral histories and unearthing family letters and legal documents that added an extra dimension to my understanding of her life. She also has a wonderful tangelo tree at her home in Gilbert, and shares its juicy fruit with John and me whenever she comes to Elgin to review the work in progress. Needless to say, this caused us to anticipate her visits with double enthusiasm!

The most unexpected and treasured find came almost at the end of the writing process, when Janet came across an old handwritten diary among her mother's things. It dated back to 1914 and recorded her great-grandfathers' two trips to visit his daughter in Arizona. His words resonated with his deep love of the old west, his curious and inquiring mind and his careful descriptions of everything and everyone he came across on his travels. His recollections gave me a deeper understanding of the lure of the west that so attracted his daughter and led to her lifetime love of this area and her vow to never leave it.

Marka Collie Moss, who is descended from a long line of pioneers on both sides of her family, has long been one of my most dedicated and reliable resources on the history of this area. She patiently answered my many questions over the years and I am eternally grateful that she was able to tell me about her memories of the Fraizers. It was her last interview before her passing in early 2017, at the age of 93, and as usual she came up with some priceless tales which added a few humorous asides to our story.

Posy Piper has been another reliable resource for many years. She treated Janet Thompson and myself to a private trip through the archives of the Cowbelles Heritage Center and spent hours helping us research photos and written accounts that were a great help in piecing together Carrie's commitment to her community.

Henry Dojaquez, another longtime member of the local community and a well-known vaquero whose help was indispensable to Carrie especially after the death of her husband, shared his memories of many round-ups on her homestead that added immensely to my understanding of Carrie's cattle ranching skills. Not to mention the fact that he is really fun to listen to as he spins his tales and chuckles along at his own jokes.

I was truly fortunate to have the assistance of three dedicated proofreaders and editors. Joe Quiroga's knowledge of all things cattle-related was invaluable in helping me to relate Carrie's ranching activities accurately. Tom Rogos' expertise in grammar and his keen eye for typographical errors prevented many of my mistakes from making it to press. The errors that remain are mine alone. Cheryl Rogos' beautiful photographs helped to visually enhance parts of the story where no old photos were available. Cheryl loves to learn the back story behind every incident, and her curiosity regarding the Church of the Brethren led to the discovery that some disagreements in the 1880s, precipitated three Brethren spinoff groups; Quakers, Mennonites and the sect that Carrie's father was connected with, German Baptist. Thanks to Cheryl, I have learned to dig a little deeper.

My deepest gratitude to my husband, John, who is always the first to look over my work before I have the courage to share it with anyone else. He notices things that I tend to gloss over, tells me honestly when the narrative is getting sidetracked, and puts up with my preoccupation when I am deep into each new story. I couldn't have written this book without his support.

Unless otherwise indicated, all the photos on the following pages are courtesy of the Fraizer family: Jim Rowley, Janet Thompson and Lynn Kelley.

Foreword

Arizona's eastern Santa Cruz County, a lush corridor of rolling grasslands, natural springs and heavily wooded mountains, extends southward from the Pima County line to the Mexican border. Panoramic mountain vistas stretch from the majestic Santa Rita Mountains at its western edge to the Huachucas and Whetstones in the east.

The first European to enter Arizona was Spanish explorer Fray Marcos de Niza, accompanied by the Moorish slave, Estavanico, who came north from Mexico in search of the Seven Cities of Cibola. When Estavanico was killed by Indians in a pueblo in present-day New Mexico in 1539, de Niza fled back to Mexico, abandoning his quest. The following year, Francisco Vasquez Coronado traveled as far east as Kansas in a vain search for the same nonexistent Cibola. Almost a century later, Father Eusebio Francisco Kino, a Jesuit missionary and explorer, entered Arizona from Mexico through the San Rafael Valley, continued over the Canelo Pass to the Babacomari River, near present day Elgin, where the Pima Indian tribe known as the Huachucas, cultivated fields along the creek.

In an attempt to encourage settlement in the area, Spain established several large land grants, including the San Ignacio del Babacomari. After the Mexican government won its independence from the Spanish crown in 1822, the new government continued the policy of establishing land grants. In 1829, Don Ignacio Elias and Doña Eulalia Elias purchased approximately 130,000 acres of the Babacomari, built a fortified ranch headquarters and raised thousands of cattle over the next 18

Carrie, Rhoda and Esther Swigart pose for a formal portrait in Philadelphia. Esther married Bruce Rothrock, homesteaded near Elgin and persuaded her two single sisters to come west to get in on the government's handout of free land. Ca. 1910.

years. The Apaches, in a series of raids killed two of the Elias brothers, stole many cattle and ransacked the hacienda, forcing the Elias family to return to Arizpe, Sonora, in 1849.

Many of the land grants were deserted by the end of the Civil War. Squatters moved in, built homes and ran cattle, although they could not get legal title to the land. Eventually Dr. E. B. Perrin, a former Confederate physician, built a successful career as a land speculator, first in California then Arizona, where he purchased title to the Babacomari in 1902 from the Elias family, forced the squatters to leave their ranches and began running cattle.

When the U.S. Forest Service was organized, it included much of the public lands in the southwest, including the grazing areas of the land grants. The government decided that a portion of the Babacomari was worth homesteading, so they eliminated it from the forest and families flocked to the area to get title to what was basically free land. In 1910, an opportunist named Beebe homesteaded in the Elgin area and started advertising far and wide, offering to meet prospective settlers at the train, take the visitors to his home and show them available parcels until they found one they liked, all for a fee of $150. Many bit at the prospect of 160 acres of free land and by the time sisters Carrie and Rhoda Swigart arrived in the area, the only free land still unclaimed was open for homesteading, but was not yet available for filing.

The Swigarts had boarded a train in Philadelphia, transferred to the westbound train in Washington, D.C., and began their journey to Arizona in 1913. They knew they had to change trains in Benson to get to the small town of Elgin which lay on the train route to Nogales, Arizona. Not being familiar with Spanish pronunciation, Carrie asked everyone she could find along the way how to get from Benson to "No gales," saying the name as if it were a calm place with no winds. Not surprisingly, no one was able to help her. Finally, in El Paso, the stationmaster said, "You must mean Nogales. It's the Spanish word for walnuts. The town is named for the trees that line the banks of the Santa Cruz River."

That was the first of what were to become many new challenging experiences as these two single women staked out their claims and planted the crops required to "prove up" on the land. The challenges were many. There was no water, electricity, roads, or access to groceries. They did not even have a horse to provide transportation. Their story is one of courage, perseverance, hard work and the independent spirit that is the hallmark of the many pioneers who paved the way for future generations to enjoy the community life that their efforts made possible.

V.P. Hanson operated the general store close to the Elgin train depot, a popular spot for arriving homesteaders in the early 1900s. Two unidentified children stand by the front door. The two-story Elgin Hotel, which later burned down, is in the background. (Photo courtesy Monta Carol Morgan and Empire Ranch Foundation.)

Chapter One

The Journey West

Carrie and Rhoda Swigart leaped to their feet and eagerly pressed their faces against the window as the Southern Pacific's "mixed train" slowly chugged into Elgin and pulled to a stop near the depot. They were seated in the lone dusty, wooden passenger car that brought up the rear of a long line of freight cars, a combination which caused it to be called a mixed train. They couldn't wait for their first glimpse of the "always sunny" Arizona town described to them in glowing terms by their little sister Esther. To their dismay, however, on this blustery March day in 1913, it was so cold and windy not even their heavy eastern coats could ward off the chill.

Carrie was the first to spot their welcoming committee, Esther's husband Bruce and his father Oliver Rothrock, who were waving vigorously from their vantage point next to Oliver's large horse-drawn freight wagon. The sisters hastily gathered together their carry-on possessions and hopped down the steps. In the excitement of finally arriving at their destination, the road-weariness of their five-day journey seemed to magically fall from their shoulders.

All during that freezing, blustery winter in Pennsylvania, Carrie, unmarried at age 31, and her sister Rhoda, who was eleven years older and also single, had been inundated with letters from Esther urging them to come to Arizona. There was still time to get in on the handout of free public land the government was offering on a first-come, first-served basis. Esther and Bruce, along with his parents, had already filed on homesteads about six miles west of the little town of Elgin near Fruitland Cemetery, and although happy, Esther was homesick and eager for her sisters to join her.

The sisters were worried that two town-bred girls like themselves would find it very difficult to build a home in the wilds of the newly formed state of Arizona, but they were bored with their life and their perfectly ordinary but tedious jobs in Philadelphia. The deciding factor, in addition to Pennsylvania's horrendous weather, was Esther's recent telegram reporting that there were only two or three available parcels left. Unless they came to Arizona right away, they would lose their chance.

With the prospect of this once-in-a-lifetime opportunity slipping from their grasp, Carrie and Rhoda decided to burn their bridges and leave as soon as possible. In the back of their minds was a fallback plan - if things didn't

Carrie Swigart in 1897, about age 16. After earning a teaching degree from Juniata College, Carrie taught for a few years before realizing that a future spent in a classroom held absolutely no appeal for her. She then enrolled in business classes at the Pierce School and obtained a position as a legal secretary with a promising young Philadelphia lawyer, Franklin Spencer Edmonds.

Rhoda Swigart in 1886 at age 14. Rhoda also had a teaching degree and taught school for a few years. She went on to nursing school and obtained a nursing degree and a well-paying job in a Philadelphia hospital. She had saved $3,000 over the years, which helped pay to drill a well on her property when she homesteaded in Arizona.

work out in Arizona, they could always continue on to California where they knew they would be able to find employment, since Rhoda was a registered nurse and Carrie had good secretarial skills.

As the train continued on its way towards Nogales, Bruce and Oliver made quick work of loading the sisters' considerable amount of luggage into the wagon. The girls had stuffed every trunk and suitcase they could find with all their possessions - clothes, linens, cooking utensils and dishes. They had even purchased canvas chairs and cots, since they knew the Rothrocks had no extra beds for guests. These precious necessities were too bulky to fit in their trunks, so they tied them with a strap and slung them over their shoulders to carry on the train. They also carried a large tin breadbox that their mother, Elizabeth, had packed with sandwiches and cookies to sustain them on the trip, since there was no food service provided on the train.

Along the trail from the depot to the Rothrock's home, the beautiful sight of Mount Wrightson, known locally as Baldy, rose majestically in the west. At that moment, Carrie made a vow to herself that she would never die happy without reaching its summit. Several years later, pregnant with her first child, Carrie scaled Baldy on the back of her horse, realizing her dream. (Cheryl Rogos photo.)

When all the luggage was safely tied down, Oliver clucked up the horses and they set out for the Rothrocks' home. Esther with her new baby was happily awaiting their arrival and after a joyful reunion, they sat down to their first home-cooked meal in Arizona. The hours sped by that evening as they happily made plans for showing Carrie and Rhoda around the area and looking over the two parcels still available for homesteading. When they finally turned in for the night, the sisters' heads were spinning with all the possibilities. Their dreams for the future were beginning to seem like more than just dreams, possibly even reality.

Sisters Carrie and Rhoda Swigart erected their first living quarters straddling the line between their two homesteads. They set up their cots on opposite sides of the tent to "prove up" both properties while living together in safety. When an official survey was conducted a few months later, it revealed that they were actually both on the same side of the line, but by that time they had staked both claims successfully. 1913.

Chapter Two
Staking the Claim

The next morning they went to look at the two sites that were still available. They were adjacent to each other, about six miles southwest of the Rothrocks' place, on the south side of the Babacomari Land Grant. This land grant, a part of the Gadsden Purchase, was about 15 miles long and three miles wide, and was unavailable for homesteading. The two available parcels Rothrock showed them were not yet open for filing on as a homestead, so the only way to secure them was to physically take possession and remain there as a squatter for three years.

The Homestead Act required that they plant crops until they obtained title to the land, but this acreage was not especially suited for farming. Since Carrie and Rhoda only planned to farm for the minimum amount of time, they did not see this as a problem. The beautiful rolling grasslands dotted with scrub oaks, which provided panoramic views of the mountains in every direction, more than made up for the lack of tillable land to their way of thinking. But still, they were undecided whether to stay or continue on to California.

A few days later, Jim Fraizer, another homesteader in the area, stopped by the Rothrocks' home and told them that he had seen two families getting off the train in Elgin. The new arrivals intended to claim these last available parcels the following morning. According to Fraizer, the only way for Carrie and Rhoda to secure the parcels for themselves was to get there ahead of the newcomers. Jim's homestead was immediately adjacent to these parcels and, as it turned out later, had an ulterior (but benevolent) motive to delivering this message urgent terms.

Faced with the prospect of losing this chance, the group leaped into action, all thoughts of the California fallback option fading into the background. They loaded up Oliver's big wagon with bedding, their precious cots and chairs, a few pans, a coffee pot, and a loaf of homemade bread, along with bacon and eggs. Oliver's colt had never been harnessed before, but he hitched him up along with the mare, and by four p.m. they were ready to set out for the property. Esther was disappointed that she was not able to accompany them, but she couldn't bring her new baby along on this nighttime trip.

Darkness fell within an hour, and before long the horses got hung up on a large century plant. With a lot of work and the judicious use of an axe, Bruce and Oliver were finally able to get the horses free, and they continued on their journey. The object of their quest was to locate a surveyor's stake, the Federal Government's official section marker, which marked off the line between claims. It measured only two feet high and three inches across.

There were no roads or fences to help guide their way, but the stars were

United States General Land Office Survey stake dated 1912 is two feet high and three inches across. Oliver Rothrock was able to locate it nestled in the tall grass in the dark of night, March, 1913. The stake is still in the same spot in this photo, taken in 2016. (Cheryl Rogos photo.)

unbelievably bright. In fact Venus, off to the west, seemed like a small moon, and the Canille (now known as Canelo) Hills helped provide a landmark to go by. Mr. Rothrock was familiar with the area as he frequented it on firewood cutting expeditions and, against all odds, he located the tiny post in that vast sea of tall grass a little before midnight.

Carrie and Rhoda set up their cots, one on the east and the other on the west side of the peg, while Bruce and his father unhitched the team and slept on the ground a short distance away. The next morning the sisters prepared bacon and eggs and enjoyed their first breakfast on their own land. Years later, Carrie was surprised to find the remains of the egg shells at the spot.

When the single men of the area heard the remarkable news that two unmarried women had staked a claim in Elgin, they hurried to the spot bearing gifts, including a Dutch oven (see the cast iron pot at the center of photo), which literally saved their lives, according to Carrie. Whenever they were able to snare a rabbit they used that oven to concoct a savory stew. The man who gave it to them left the area before they could properly thank him, leaving the oven behind. Carrie considered it one of her treasured possessions for many years.

Chapter Three

Single Women

After breakfast, Bruce and Oliver went over the hill to Ike Fraizer's homestead to water their horses and pen them up for a spell. According to Carrie's memoirs, "They advertised our arrival, so by 10 a.m. we had a lot of help!" Most of the homesteaders up to that time were bachelors, and every unmarried man for miles around was racing to be the first to check out these single women.

They came bearing many useful gifts including a tent, an axe, several loads of wood, a cooking pot and a large piece of canvas. Someone hauled in a barrel of water and another man fashioned little posts and strung wire to build a fence around their tent. Their most prized gift was a Dutch oven that literally saved their lives, according to Carrie. She said she never got skilled at baking biscuits, they were usually burned or half baked, but they ate them and lived. Helping them get settled, in addition to the Rothrocks, were the three Fraizer brothers, Ike, Charlie and Jim; the two Yeary boys, Gus and Earl; and John McCarty to name a few.

The men stepped off what they thought was their corner and called that their imaginary line. They set up the tent on one side. It was just big enough for their two cots with a narrow center aisle between them. They stretched the large piece of canvas over two poles and hung a few pans underneath, to serve as a makeshift kitchen.

When the newcomers arrived later in the morning, the Swigarts were already settled in. Fortunately, the disappointed strangers left right away without surveying the parcel. Some months later when the official survey was completed, they discovered that they had placed everything on the same side of the line, but by that time, their claims for both parcels were securely in place.

The rolling hills were lush with grass that some claimed was high as a horse's belly, and it was feared that their cooking fires might cause a blaze. One of the men suggested that they burn it off. Instead of setting one fire with a lookout guarding it, they set fires on both sides of the camp and soon a gust of wind came up igniting a raging inferno. It crept under the horses' legs and singed the canvas and their bedding. It was nightfall before it reached a spot where they could control it and put it out. Carrie was later embarrassed because as she said, "We were always known as the girls that set the grass on fire, even though we hadn't really done it."

That night after everyone left the two girls were totally alone in the wilderness, without even a light to brighten up their dark camp. About five miles away they could barely make out a tiny pinpoint of light. There was no water nearby, so no birds to lighten up the atmosphere. It was so quiet that Carrie thought she could hear the blood circulating in her ears. She remembered it as the only time that she was ever really discouraged and she couldn't help but wonder what the future would bring.

The next morning they were welcomed by a glorious sunrise spreading over the mountains to the east. That sight put their minds at rest, and they felt reassured that they had made the right decision. They patched up the burned canvas, salvaged what bedding they could and started in housekeeping.

From day one, they had a steady stream of gentlemen callers. They fed first-time visitors, but were very careful to remain "circumspect." If one of the men starting taking advantage he got the cold shoulder. Over the following weeks, someone would stop by with a piece of beef or a freshly shot rabbit and he would always be willing to stay and help eat it. However, Carrie said they were good at getting them to chop firewood to cook the meal.

With all the hard work they had to do, Carrie and Rhoda soon resorted to wearing overalls. Years later, Ilene Fraizer said that her mother-in-law much preferred Arizona, where a girl could even wear pants, to the straight-laced existence in Philadelphia. Their more sedate neighbors criticized their attire, but with all the stickers and thistles in the pastures they thought "to heck with the snooty neighbors," and wore the pants anyway.

The girls felt they were fairly notorious with the local prim and proper married women, but they were very careful. As Carrie remarked, "At age 32 and 43, we were old enough to know what it was all about. I don't think we were ever criticized. Unless we knew everybody's pedigree we never allowed them inside. I will say all the men kind of dressed up in their best when they came to see us. They'd come with their white collars on, even their best clothes."

Eva "Ma" Barnett lived in the Southern Pacific station house in Elgin after her husband who had been stationmaster, passed away. She took in railroad workers as roomers and served as "ex officio" stationmaster. Dubbed the "Belle of Elgin" in this postcard, Barnett leans on the fence in front of the station house. (Photo courtesy Donnie Martin.)

Chapter Four
Necessities of Life

Exploring their new countryside became a passion and the two sisters spent many happy hours hiking over hill and dale. On one such foray, they looked around and realized that all the hills looked the same and they had no idea in which direction their tent was located. Rhoda decided to go around a hill, while Carrie took the tougher trail over the top. She ended up reaching home about two hours before Rhoda finally arrived, hot, dusty and thirsty.

At first they had nothing to cook on but a makeshift stove one of their gentlemen callers fashioned for them from an old kerosene oil can. He cut out one of the square ends and made a vent at the other end for the smoke to escape. That is how they managed to heat up their oatmeal and coffee for the first few weeks, until one day when they came upon a deserted surveyor's camp. There were parts of a cook-stove scattered across the ground including the section that the pipe fit into, along with a large oven door. They carried these pieces of heavy iron two miles back to their tent, and by digging a small hole and setting them together they fashioned a stove that performed a lot better than the kerosene oil can. With their skillet and a coffee pot and their trunk set outside to serve as a table, they could dine al fresco style.

Many ingredients for their meals were gathered from what they could find growing wild. They made jellies from wild grapes and pies using manzanita berries. The small native walnuts, although hard to pick out of the shells, made delicious cookies, and pigweed served well as a vegetable. Any groceries they purchased came by train from Maier's Store in Benson and had to be picked up right away at the Elgin Depot. Incoming deliveries were fair game. If the customer didn't get there on time to claim them they might disappear. The stationmaster, Harry Barnett, had passed away and Southern Pacific allowed his wife, "Ma," to live in the station house. She took in railroad workers as boarders and served as the "ex officio" station master, although she felt no responsibility for making sure the deliveries were passed on to the correct person.

By early May, the weather had started turning hot, and keeping their food fresh presented another challenge. An open can of milk would be sour by the next morning and eventually Carrie and Rhoda both became ill. They were too sick to go for help and so doctored each other until they finally recovered.

It wasn't long before it became obvious that even though they could "dry farm" without irrigation to fulfill their obligation for proving up the land, water was going to be their most pressing concern. There was just one well in pumping condition in the entire area, and everybody in the area went there for water. They had to pay $1 a barrel to have it hauled the three miles to their tent, as they did not yet have any way to transport it themselves. The cost made it prohibitive to buy enough water to do the laundry, as the precious liquid had to be rationed for more important uses such as drinking, cooking and bathing. With their outdoor way of life, dirty clothes mounted up quickly. They needed to figure out something soon.

Their solution was to strap the bundles of dirty clothes on their backs and walk the six miles to Bruce and Esther's house where they spent the night. The following morning they would strap the bundles on their backs again, this time with the addition of Esther's and the baby's laundry, and walk another mile to Oliver Rothrock's place. Oliver had drilled a well, but did not have enough money at that time for a windmill, so they had to haul the water up by a windlass, one bucket at a time, for almost 200 feet. It took all day to complete the task, do the wash and then load up the clean clothes and walk back to Esther's to spend another night.

Early the following morning they would set out for the six mile walk back, to be sure they would get home before dark. Once night fell, they would have nothing to guide their way but the outline of the hills. Their home lay against a rounded hill in the distance and they feared they would miss the one fold in the hills that contained their tent. If they could find the cow path that led up their draw for about a mile, they would be safe. Carrie said they always found the path, and even though they were just living in a canvas tent, it was furnished with their

The well at Oliver Rothrock's homestead. Esther and two of her children, unloading melons, are near the freight wagon her father-in-law, Oliver, brought with him from Chico, California. Oliver with Prince, his prize-winning Morgan, is standing next to the well where Carrie and Rhoda hauled up buckets of water to do their laundry. 1913.

precious cots and to them it was home.

Transportation was becoming increasingly important to them and soon they were able to purchase a small mustang mare and colt for $35 from a man named White who lived in Sonoita. Mr. White even threw in a little wagon and a harness, so now they could haul their water themselves. They got four empty beer kegs from a bar at Fairbank and used them to haul the water the three miles from the well to their home. The mare turned out to be rather balky and if she decided to stop and rest a mile from home, she couldn't be persuaded to continue onward. Carrie thought she could cure this behavior by tying her to a pole and leaving her all night. When she untied her the following morning the mare hurried home lickety-split, but she never kicked the bad habit, remaining stubborn to the end of her days.

Carrie found a small saddle to fit the mare and spent many an enjoyable hour exploring the surrounding hillsides. One day she rode her into a pond to get a drink and the horse waded out to the middle and lay down. Carrie jumped off just as the horse went down and she ended up standing in water and mud up to her waist.

Soon she acquired Bill, the first of what was to become many cats. She told people Bill was not a common cat, but a human being who just didn't speak English. He loved to ride up on the saddle with her and she took him everywhere, from a day's ride to haul water to a trip to Esther's for a visit. One morning hearing a noise outside, she went to investigate and found the cat already mounted and ready to ride. He had run up the horse's leg and was sitting in the saddle eagerly waiting for the next day's adventure to begin.

After Carrie got the little mare, she rode to the Post Office at Elgin one day and stayed too long talking to the neighbors and catching up on the national and local news. When the train arrived, the railroad men brought word from the outside world and also delivered the Kansas City Star, a favorite paper with the homesteaders, which sparked many discussions and made for a stimulating social hour. She had such an interesting afternoon that it was nearly sunset by the time she started for home. Then the sky clouded over. She said it was so dark she couldn't see the grass at the horse's feet and the skyline had disappeared. There are deep ditches in the draws from erosion and she had to trust the horse to avoid them. Finally the little mare stopped, and there was the gate into the enclosure outside her house.

Bill, the first cat that Carrie got in Arizona, loved to go horseback riding with her. One day she came outside to find him already in the saddle, waiting for the day's adventure to begin.

Jim Fraizer erected this one-room house for Carrie soon after she moved to the property, according to a note written on the back of the photo years later by her son, Sam Fraizer. Carrie can be seen looking through the window and Rhoda is standing at the door in the snow. Late 1913.

Chapter Five

Proving Up

The sisters' original plan was to build one house straddling the line, with a bedroom on each side of the claims and a living room and kitchen in the middle. As it turned out it was fortunate that they didn't build at once, because when the heat of summer hit they definitely changed their minds.

Their claims adjoined for only one quarter of a mile, and the hills rose rather steeply on each side of what is known as a draw. A short distance to the west and up a steep rise there was a beautiful oak tree. They spent their summer days there in the shade of the oak and finally decided that would be the perfect place to build the first house, which would be Carrie's home.

By this time, they realized it would be more comfortable to build two houses, each on a hill, rather than sweltering through the summer in "an oven," as Carrie referred to their original site. They had not yet officially filed on the land, but had decided which land each one would have. They were both happy with their choices. Carrie's parcel, on the west side, had the most trees while Rhoda chose the more open ground and the better building site to the east. Rhoda built her house within calling distance and they ate their meals together, but still had their privacy.

The lumber to build the house was hauled from Benson to the site of their tent. Jim Fraizer was more than happy to build the dwelling for them, but he was committed to other jobs for the next several weeks. While they waited for him to get freed up, the two of them singlehandedly carried every bit of the lumber up the hill on foot to the newly chosen site. They got up early each morning, carried several loads of lumber, took a break for breakfast, and then carried a few more loads. In the evening they started again until finally they had it all up on the hill.

At the time the Swigarts arrived, each homesteader was allowed to claim a maximum of 160 acres. The following year, the government increased the limit to 320 acres per settler. The first arrivals to the area were allowed to add on to their original acreage, but soon most of the excess land was allocated. As latecomers, Rhoda and Carrie were happy to be able to increase their parcels to a total of 260 acres each. To comply with the law, homesteaders had to farm a certain number of acres, an increasing amount each year. Since the property they were on was not yet open for filing they were still considered squatters, but their time living there and planting crops counted towards their homesteading requirements.

The first year they put in pinto beans, but the ground was so full of clods they had trouble cultivating their crop. There was no irrigation so, as Carrie put it, "What grew, grew." They put in four acres of beans that year and Carrie pulled them all and thrashed them out that fall. The following year they planted about ten acres and again, Carrie pulled them all and beat them out on a canvas. Rhoda got headaches from all the stooping, so she did the housework for both of them while Carrie, who much preferred working outdoors, tended the crops by herself. The next year they were fortunate to have the help of farm laborers from Mexico to pull and beat out the beans.

They raised mila maize (a type of corn) and pinto beans, which they later sold by the ton. All the homesteaders made their money from the beans as it was the only money crop. No one except the large ranches like the Empire and the Rail X raised cattle at that time. It was all open range with nothing fenced, and the cattle ranged as far away as Ft. Huachuca, near Fry, now known as Sierra Vista.

They bought their groceries from B. Maier in Benson. Maier allowed homesteaders to run a tab until their crops came in and they were able to pay off their grocery bill. "If you couldn't pay it off within a year, he would give you another year," Carrie told an interviewer. "This country could never have been populated without B. Maier. He trusted everybody for a year's credit and then he would buy your crops and give you a good price for it. I am sure we didn't make expenses, but we had the time of our lives doing it." Maier Brothers Store, on the corner of Fourth Street and San Pedro Street in Benson, burned to the ground in 1921.

The second year, Carrie and Rhoda separated their two properties and each

Albern Dalton helped Carrie and Rhoda plow their land. He and his wife, Lorena, raised dairy cows and delivered milk from their homestead in Elgin to Nogales. To keep the milk fresh, they kept thick-walled iceboxes in this building called the milk house. The ice came from C. B. "Chris" Wilson's ice plant in Patagonia. Laundry was done on the little open porch on the back. The Daltons later moved to Nogales where they operated a dairy on the Old Nogales Highway. Their daughter, Hettie Lee, served as assistant postmistress at Sonoita when the new post office building was dedicated in 1962. (Photo courtesy Monta Carol Morgan and Bowman Archives Center).

plowed her own land, with the help of a neighbor, Albern Dalton. Dalton and his wife Lorena raised dairy cows and delivered milk from their homestead in Elgin to Nogales.

One day about six weeks after Jim Fraizer erected the little one-room house for her, Carrie had a visitor who was a little scary. Rhoda, a trained nurse, had gone to Rothrocks' for a few days to help with Esther's sick baby leaving Carrie alone, when suddenly, there came a knock on the door. Tiny Carrie, only five feet tall, tentatively opened the door to find a huge man, measuring well over six feet, wearing a ten-gallon hat over his long bushy hair. His whiskers seemed to start at his hat and go all the way down into his collar. His outfit was topped off by a leather vest, chaps and high cowboy boots. He stood there staring at her without saying a word.

Carrie was so frightened that she said later she would have shot him if she'd had a gun. He finally said, "I'm looking for my bull." Carrie opened the door wide to show him the empty room and said, "Well, I don't have him." With that she slammed and locked the door. He was later identified as Clyde McPherson, a cowboy from the San Rafael Valley, who although already married, had ridden ten miles across the mountain to have a look at the Swigart girls who were causing such a local sensation.

This was during the time of Pancho Villa and the sisters were concerned about the bands of revolutionaries in his service who came across the border at will. Rhoda built a barn on her property and dragged a double bed, out there. All one summer the two sisters slept there with a gun beside them. It made them feel safer, although they were never actually bothered by anyone.

The only time Carrie ever ran into the revolutionaries was one day when she decided to ride over by Papago Springs, just south of current day Sonoita, on her newly acquired horse. There were no border fences at that time and only 75 Immigration Service Agents patrolled the entire border from El Paso, Texas to California, compared to today, when upwards of 17,000 U.S. Border Patrol agents keep watch over the same area. As Carrie topped a small hill she suddenly came upon a camp of about 50 Mexicans who were as surprised to see her as she was to see them. Villa's men started to yell excitedly when they saw it was a woman approaching. She hastily spurred her little mustang and said later that she never knew her horse could run as fast as he did getting out of there.

Betty Barr

Samuel and Elizabeth Swigart's farm in Lewiston, Pennsylvania, where Carrie and Rhoda grew up. Their father was also a minister and circuit rider for the Church of the Brethren. Carrie said that her Pennsylvania Dutch heritage inclined the sisters to be thrifty. Rhoda had saved almost $3,000 from her years of working as a nurse. Carrie had about half that much, since she was younger and had not had a paying job for as long a time.

Chapter Six

Visitors From Home

In June of 1914 Carrie's parents, Samuel and Elizabeth Swigart, set out from their home in Pennsylvania and traveled across the northern part of the United States to Seattle to attend a religious conference, preaching along the way when invited by the congregation. Samuel was a Baptist minister, a circuit rider for the Church of the Brethren in Central Pennsylvania. The church had gone through a tumultuous period in the 1880s and separated into three distinct groups. The Quakers and Mennonites were the most well-known. Samuel adhered to the tenets of the German Baptist group.

On the way, they had stopped in Oregon to visit many of their friends and relatives who had relocated there. At the conclusion of the convention, the couple extended their journey to southeastern Arizona to visit their three daughters. Samuel kept a detailed journal of their trip, noting the changing scenery, types of wildlife and trees, the people they met and their various adventures.

"We arrived at the train station in Elgin at noon on July 4, 1914," he wrote, "and found everybody (underlined) watching for us. We ate dinner all together at Esther's and then Carrie and Rhoda went home and we stayed at Esther's."

Their visit lasted until August 31, and it is evident from Samuel's notes that he was not only delighted to be reunited, at least for a short time, with three of his nine children, but that he also had a keen eye for detail. If he saw an interesting cactus, he noted the dimensions. One of his favorites was a huge saguaro that

Samuel and Elizabeth Swigart with their nine surviving children. Front row: Unknown child, Samuel James Swigart, Esther Catherine, Elizabeth Rupert Swigart. Back row: Probably James William,

Rhoda Mae, Mary Jane, probably Christian Hanawalt and John Goodman, unknown child, Carrie Rebecca. Two other children died at early ages, Martha, age 7 and Ella age 17 months. 1895.

Samuel and Elizabeth Swigart with their youngest child, Esther Rothrock, at the Rothrock's Elgin homestead in 1914.

Elizabeth and Samuel Swigart on horseback at Esther and Bruce's homestead. 1914.

Sisters Rhoda, Carrie and Esther Swigart with an unknown man, possibly one of their brothers, enjoying the beach on the Jersey shore.

Esther Swigart at 16 months and Carrie Swigart at six years of age.

The picnic area south of Patagonia where the family camped overnight and picked elderberries. They slept on a "floor used for dancing that was set in a grove of large trees along a fine stream of water," according to Samuel's journal entry. Front row from left: Bruce Rothrock and his daughter, Marie; Carrie Swigart holding two of her many cats. Back row Elizabeth Swigart, Jim Fraizer, Samuel Swigart, Esther Rothrock, John McCarty and Rhoda Swigart. 1914.

he judged was at least 20 feet high, "The greatest I have ever seen." When he looked at a mountain, he estimated the altitude. On sightseeing trips, he figured the distances and the directions precisely.

The second day of their visit, the Rothrocks planned an overnight camping trip and picnic at a scenic spot about 22 miles south of Patagonia. Carrie and Rhoda invited Jim Fraizer and John McCarty, who by this time had become their constant visitors, to join them. They had heard that the elderberries were ripe for picking and wanted to bring home as much as they could. They planned to eat some now and can the rest so they could be enjoyed during the long winter ahead. Samuel noted that the grove, "lies between huge rock-covered peaks and the enormous flatland contains rolling grasslands and is for sale at $500 per acre because of its rich mineral deposits."

The following Sunday, Esther and Bruce and Oliver's family all attended Sunday school at the one-room Rain Valley Schoolhouse. Samuel was pleased to be invited to preach the bible class and give a sermon at the end of the services. No slacker, Samuel made himself useful during his stay. He helped with all the chores including hauling water, installing a drain spout on Carrie's house, staking Rhoda's newly acquired parcel, cutting firewood, and planting alongside his daughters. He even made picture frames for the family photos the girls treasured.

On July 17, he noted that the rains were so heavy the girls were assured their crops were now safe. Samuel had brought cots with him and he and Elizabeth slept at Carrie's and the next day helped plant peas, turnips and radishes. He noted that the corn was coming in tassels and pumpkins and melons were developing. However, one month later a huge hail storm damaged the beans and corn crop. The elder Swigarts, sleeping in a tent outside Carrie's house, were rained out. The roof of the tent leaked and they were forced to sleep on the floor, but they seemed to cope with all challenges that came their way.

One of their favorite excursions during this visit was a trip their daughters arranged to see the cave at Papago Springs that Carrie had explored a few months previously when she had run into Pancho Villa's troops. The whole family went – Carrie and her parents

The cave at Papago Springs which was "rediscovered" in 1934 by Quentin Roosevelt, grandson of President Theodore Roosevelt, and his friend, Joseph Burden. The two came to Sonoita and stayed at the Los Encinos Guest Ranch operated by Neil Carr and his wife. They discovered a small bone projecting from the ceiling on their way out of the cave, returned the next day and found two skulls, a pelvis and some vertebrae and numerous limb bones. They sent the fragments to the American Museum of Natural History and received notice that the bones appeared to be from a prehistoric animal similar to the American pronghorn. (Betty Barr photo.)

drove in a wagon with Esther's daughter Marie. Rhoda and Esther rode beside them on horseback. Bruce Rothrock was already in the area cutting wood for posts and was able to take a break and join them for a picnic lunch.

The final sightseeing trip the elder Swigarts undertook on this visit was to the Biscuit, a favorite local landmark that rises majestically seven miles east of Sonoita in the Mustang Mountain Range, on the way to Fairbank and Tombstone. The family trekked to the summit and, as was his custom, Samuel recorded his measurements of the hill and his impressions of the stupendous 180 degree view of the countryside.

The following day, Samuel and Elizabeth reluctantly begin the chore of packing up their belongings in preparation for the journey homeward. Oliver Rothrock arrived early on the morning of August 31 to transport them to the train station in his surrey. His son Bruce loaded up all their luggage in the freight wagon and followed along behind. The entry in Samuels' journal recorded his feelings on leaving his three daughters and the land he had come to love. "What a parting. How sad for loved ones to separate. But such is life."

Betty Barr

Brothers Jim (left) and Charlie Fraizer in front of Jim's dugout shack in Elgin around 1910 with an unidentified child. The roof was constructed of sagging green oak poles topped by a layer of bear grass. A door and window completed the amenities. To keep out the rain, Jim hung a large dishwater tub over his bed. (Photo courtesy Ilene Fraizer and Marka Moss).

Chapter Seven

Romance on the Range

It wasn't long before Carrie and Rhoda started to think about which of their many suitors they would marry.

It all began for Carrie with a dinner invitation from one of the three bachelor brothers who was homesteading nearby. Jim Fraizer, originally from Rolla, Missouri, had arrived in the area in 1907 along with his brothers, Isaac (Ike) and Charlie. Jim was a carpenter by trade, Charlie was a bricklayer, and Ike had a Bachelor of Science degree in civil engineering.

The combination of three grown men living together in close quarters soon led to quarrels and Jim, the middle one in age, moved to a dugout he had built under a hill. This was the "home" where Carrie and Rhoda were to be served dinner.

The sisters couldn't help but be taken aback at Jim's living arrangements. The roof of the dugout was constructed of green oak poles that sagged in the middle when they dried out. The poles were covered with dirt that had bear grass growing out of it. The roof leaked during rainstorms and to keep dry, Jim tied a large dishpan to the poles that hung over an old mattress he slept on. A homemade table was flanked with sawhorses that provided uncomfortable seating.

For dinner, Jim prepared his famous biscuits. To make sure they were baked all the way through he let them brown on top, then flipped them over and browned them on the other side. The front of the dugout was graced with a door and a window. The stovepipe stuck out the window and didn't draw well, so by the time the biscuits were getting done, the room had filled up with smoke.

Despite this inauspicious beginning, Carrie eventually accepted Jim's proposal of marriage. Then the Government stepped in to throw a monkey wrench in their plans. The rules stated that each person had to live on his own parcel for at least two years before filing a claim. Since the properties that Carrie and Rhoda were living on were not yet open for filing, they were considered squatters. Finally on October 1, 1915, their acreages came open for filing, approximately two and a half years after they staked their claims.

Although the time they spent growing crops counted toward their homestead requirements, a woman couldn't file on her claim after she was married because the name on the claim would be different. To comply with the regulations and be allowed to keep both homesteads, she and Jim had to decide which home-

Jim Fraizer's older brother Ike was a civil engineer and served as City of Nogales and later Santa Cruz County engineer. On September 17, 1932, front page headlines across the State of Arizona shouted the news, "Fraizer's Body Recovered From Fire Ruins." The story went on to say, "Fraizer perished in flames that broke out following a gasoline explosion at the Texaco Company gasoline storage plant in Miami, AZ. of which he was manager." When Ike left Elgin, Jim and Carrie bought his interest in the Fraizer homestead.

Jim Fraizer with his brother-in-law, Dyke Wilson who was married to Jim's sister Sarah, and one of the Wilsons' children. Photo taken in their hometown Rolla, Missouri. Ca. early 1900s.

stead they would live on, file on the claim as soon as the two years was up, and get permission from the government to marry and continue proving up afterwards. They decided to live on Jim's property since he had recently drilled a well.

"My husband thought it was a wonderful joke that he had to get permission from Washington to get married, even though he was a grown man in his thirties," Carrie said. The couple waited three weeks until October 20, to tie the knot, as that was the date of Carrie's parents' fiftieth wedding anniversary. She wrote to them saying she couldn't send them anything to commemorate their golden anniversary except "a golden son-in-law."

The minister who was to marry them lived in Rain Valley, just across the line in Pima County. This meant they had to send to Tucson for a marriage license as their homesteads were in Santa Cruz County. Carrie rode her horse to the Post Office in Elgin and asked to pick up both her mail and Jim's, but there was nothing

Phoenix 028545   4—1003-R.

The United States of America,

To all to whom these presents shall come, Greeting:

WHEREAS, a Certificate of the Register of the Land Office at **Phoenix, Arizona,** has been deposited in the General Land Office, whereby it appears that, pursuant to the Act of Congress of May 20, 1862, "To Secure Homesteads to Actual Settlers on the Public Domain," and the acts supplemental thereto, the claim of **Carrie R. Swigart Fraiser, formerly Carrie R. Swigart,** has been established and duly consummated, in conformity to law, for the **northwest quarter and the southwest quarter of the northeast quarter of Section fifteen and the Lots three and four of Section ten in Township twenty-one south of Range seventeen east of the Gila and Salt River Meridian, Arizona, containing two hundred sixty and fifty-three-hundredths acres,**

according to the Official Plat of the Survey of the said Land, returned to the GENERAL LAND OFFICE by the Surveyor-General:

NOW KNOW YE, That there is, therefore, granted by the UNITED STATES unto the said claimant the tract of Land above described; TO HAVE AND TO HOLD the said tract of Land, with the appurtenances thereof, unto the said claimant and to the heirs and assigns of the said claimant forever; subject to any vested and accrued water rights for mining, agricultural, manufacturing, or other purposes, and rights to ditches and reservoirs used in connection with such water rights, as may be recognized and acknowledged by the local customs, laws, and decisions of courts; and there is reserved from the lands hereby granted, a right of way thereon for ditches or canals constructed by the authority of the United States.

IN TESTIMONY WHEREOF, I, **Woodrow Wilson,** President of the United States of America, have caused these letters to be made Patent, and the seal of the General Land Office to be hereunto affixed.

GIVEN under my hand, in the District of Columbia, the **SIXTH** day of **JANUARY** in the year of our Lord one thousand nine hundred and **NINETEEN** and of the Independence of the United States the one hundred and **FORTY-THIRD.**

(SEAL.)

By the President: Woodrow Wilson
By M. P. LeRoy, Secretary.
John O'Connell Acting Recorder of the General Land Office.

RECORD OF PATENTS: Patent Number **657443**

Copy of Carrie's Homestead Land Grant, dated January 6, 1919, signed by President Woodrow Wilson. It lists both her maiden and married names as required by law. (Courtesy Cowbelles Ranchers' Heritage Center.)

addressed to either one of them from the Pima County Courthouse. The next day she rode the long trail back to Elgin again and this time the postmistress, Chopeta (Bartlett) Collie, reluctantly handed her the envelope she had been waiting for. It had been there the previous day, but Mrs. Collie was afraid it was bad news from the courthouse and hoping to spare Carrie she held it back, inadvertently causing Carrie two long horseback rides and a lot of anxiety. Chopeta and her husband Bill Collie were both from homesteading families. Bill's father, Reuben, was the first postmaster at Elgin, and Chopeta's parents were Marcus and Nellie Bartlett who settled nearby.

Rev. and Mrs. Samuel J. Swigart
announce the marriage of their daughter
Carrie
to
Mr. James G. Fraizer
on Tuesday, October the nineteenth
nineteen hundred and fifteen
Elgin, Arizona

Wedding announcement for Carrie Swigart and Jim Fraizer, sent out by Carrie's parents on October 19, the day before their wedding on October 20, 1915.

The following day, license in hand, Jim and Carrie hitched up his buckboard and team of mules and set out for Rain Valley. They brought their lunch in a tin tobacco can and ate it on the side of the road along the way. After saying their vows, they proceeded on to Esther and Bruce's home for a celebration and wedding dinner.

At the same time that Jim was wooing Carrie, John McCarty had his sights set on Rhoda. John, who was about six years younger than Rhoda, had come to Arizona Territory from Kansas at the age of eight in 1884. His oldest sister's husband, a man by the name of Hugo Igo, had come to the area to work on the railroad. He liked it so much he sent for his family to join him. Before long his wife's family, the McCartys, also came out and settled in Canelo, about ten miles southeast of Rhoda's homestead, where they raised cattle and had a huge fruit orchard.

Rhoda accepted John's proposal, but she was quite proud of her flock of turkeys and didn't want to be married until after she had a chance to sell them for Thanksgiving. She and John were married at the end of November, about six weeks after Jim and Carrie tied the knot.

John's family were squatters and had never filed on their property officially, so it was decided that he would move over to Rhoda's place. She had used a lot of the money saved from her work in Pennsylvania to drill a well, which was very important if they were to be able to raise cattle. John was experienced in the cattle industry as his family raised beef in Canelo, and the couple wasn't married long before they had about 50 head.

Jim and Carrie, on the other hand, knew nothing about raising cattle, although Carrie was much taken with the idea and eager to get started. Jim was more interested in the construction trade but he agreed to her plan to start a cattle business. But first they had to build a home. Carrie was definitely not going to live in the dugout.

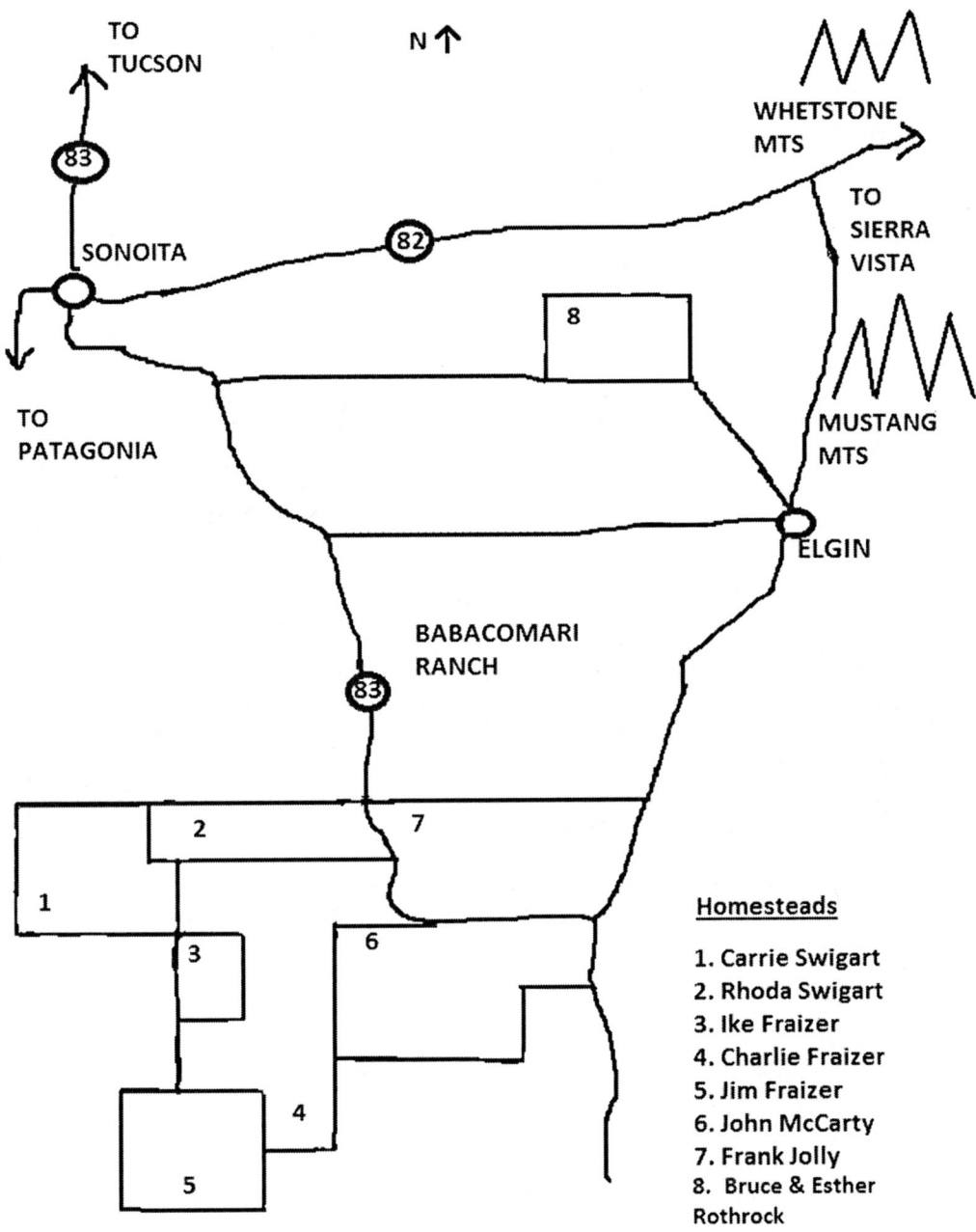

Note: State Route 83 and Interstate 10, not in existence in 1913, are shown to provide a frame of reference only. Parcels numbered 1 – 7 are located near the present-day Vaughn Loop Road. Parcel number 8 is near the Lower Elgin Road. (Map by Janet Rowley Thompson.)

Jim Fraizer and Bruce Rothrock with unidentified man in wagon, possibly Oliver Rothrock, start to work on the home Jim is building for his new wife on the Fraizer homestead.

Chapter Eight
Making a Home

Jim Fraizer set to work immediately to construct a suitable home for himself and his new wife. His first step was to tear down Carrie's house and reuse all the materials, including the nails which he painstakingly pulled out and hammered until they were straight enough to drive in. Nothing was wasted. He said he could always come up with a use for anything, and he did.

Years later his grandson Jim Rowley was exploring in the attic and found boxes of photographic plates that Jim saved. He would strip the coating off and use them to make glass for the windows.

He started the house by building a single room. As his family and their needs grew, he added on additional rooms, shotgun style. There were no hallways, each room opened into another and then another. As Carrie explained, "My husband was a wonderful mechanic and he did it all. From the very beginning he didn't like the cow business and that was the only thing that brought in real honest to goodness money. But he had plenty to do. He took care of building about 25 miles of fence."

But all was not sweetness and light. "We built the house and when they were building the porch I told him that if he built the porch without building a stone wall, I would tear the porch down. So we had really a set-to and it sat there almost a year with everything out there in the front yard ready for building a porch. Finally, I wore him down and we built a stone wall."

Now it was up to Carrie to take on the life of a ranch wife. She told of the difficulty in getting money, "There was no work for a man unless he went to Bisbee and left the family. If a man had a wife she could hold down the homestead. She could live on the ranch without him, because the mother makes the home. So, many times the man did have to go away and it was a hardship on the woman because she probably didn't even have a horse to go to town and only a few people lived near enough to walk there."

Carrie was a self-described loner. "I always had trouble making friends," she said, although she was very involved in community activities and she and Jim got together with many different friends for dinner. Jim, on the other hand, was extremely gregarious. After he put a pump on his well, neighbors came from far and wide to get water. They never charged anyone for water; that was just what neighbors did for each other. Carrie said, "The only thing was, people would come

Charles Everhart (at left) and Jim Fraizer, lifelong friends, owned homesteads close to each other. Everhart had been a switch engineer for Southern Pacific Railroad in Tucson, and had the honor of tooting a switch engine whistle February 14, 1912 when Arizona Territory became the 48th state. It was the signal for all the city to celebrate.

and they would stay all day, stay for lunch if anybody would give them any. Jim was a big talker and Mr. Everhart was a big talker and I'd stand there listening to them and see which one could tell the biggest lies. They enjoyed themselves. They should have been plowing, but after all, life passes." Charles and Cora Everhart homesteaded on a parcel adjacent to Fraizers.' He had retired as a railroad engineer

Charles and Cora Everhart at their homestead with an unknown boy riding in the back of their wagon. Cora was named Postmistress at Elgin in 1919. After she resigned that position, she taught at several schools before serving as County School Superintendent from 1942 to 1965.
(Photo courtesy Sharon Everhart Perrill.)

and ran the homestead, while Cora taught school. She eventually became Superintendent of Schools for Santa Cruz County and was a longtime volunteer secretary for the Santa Cruz County Fair and Rodeo Association.

Carrie had invested her savings in stock issued by the Pennsylvania Railroad Company, safeguarding the money to provide for hospital and funeral expenses that she might incur in the future if, as she put it, "I died an old maid." Now that she was married, she figured she could count on her husband to take care of those contingencies, so she sold the stock and used those funds to purchase their starter herd. It was difficult to find anyone willing to sell mother cows, but finally Nathanial Houston, who ranched near the West Gate to Fort Huachuca, agreed to sell her four mother cows. Fortunately, they each calved within a short period of time. "We got the bull in from the forest. He belonged to Mr. Oscar Ashburn and we called him Oscar. And he was a very nice gentle bull. He was the father of all our first calves. He (Mr. Ashburn) never knew we had him."

Carrie had been dying to have some butter, something she hadn't had a taste of since she left Pennsylvania three years previously. Range cattle are not gentle enough to be milked, so about two years after she started her cattle operation, she purchased a milk cow, and gradually increased that herd until she had about twelve dairy cows. From them she produced about 60 pounds of butter a week.

Jim would sell the butter, along with eggs from their chickens, at Fort Huachuca where he worked as a carpenter and mechanic. "One morning when he got there, he couldn't get out of the car. His appendix had burst during the night. They operated on him that afternoon. He was in the hospital two months because gangrene had set in, so I had to take over at that time." During lean times, and later when Jim was laid up in the hospital in El Paso for seven months after an auto accident, the sales from Carrie's dairy products help tide the family over till he was able to go back to work. Carrie would get up early, milk the cows, lug about 12 gallons of milk back to the house, separate it, skim off the cream and ship it by rail to California.

Carrie and Jim made some money with milk cows and then gradually went into ranching, buying up land from homesteaders who had given up. "We bought people's land. They would prove up on their land and then be so poor all they wanted to do was get rid of it, so we bought lots of land for $4 an acre, and we never paid more than $10 an acre for any of it. People were glad for any cash they could get." They also received some land in return for their kindness. For instance, their neighbor, Frank Jolly, who had no children, was so grateful for their care in his final months, that he left them the title to his homestead.

From the beginning Carrie kept a ledger book where she recorded the names of each cow, starting with the letter A and continuing through the alphabet all the way to Z. Another column contained a description of the cow's markings, the names of all her calves and their markings, and the dates the steers were sold. One of her favorites was named V, for Vivian. Once she reached the end of the alphabet, she started over again, finding a new name beginning with A and so on. She always said the hardest names to come up with were ones beginning with X and Z.

Over her long ranching career she filled two huge ledgers with hundreds of names and descriptions of every animal she owned. The first entry is dated Nov. 29, 1915, when she purchased nine cows, varying in price from $10 for Rose to

$45 for Moolie. Rose was sold Oct. 14, 1929 for $50, but Moolie died July 10, 1921 according to the book. The last entries, posted in November and December, 1973, were the results of cattle sales. Carrie's grandson, Jim Rowley remembered she filled two thick, cloth-covered books, one gray and the other burgundy, with her records. She even drew a picture of each new baby, complete with the little face and ears and all its markings. The books have long been missing, but a partial list of names has survived.

Some of Carrie's Cows
Listed in Alphabetical Order

Blue	Mary
Candy	Matilda
Coues	Moolie
Dixie	Nora Beth
Eleanor	Patsy
Flossy	Penelope
Grace	Polly
Georgette	Priscilla
Grandmother	Rosie
Ilene	Sara
Ivory	Smart
Janet	Terry
Johnny Yuma	Vivian

She often named cows after friends and relatives. At round-up time, she would look over the range and point out Nora Beth, named for Nora Beth (Smith) Aycock, or Ilene, named in honor of her daughter-in-law Ilene Fraizer, to the crews helping with gatherings or doctoring. If she didn't see the cow she wanted, she would refer to her ledger and tell the cowboy what markings to look for. Since she ran a cow-calf operation, most of the names were female; however she did keep a few bulls. Oscar, who fathered her first four calves, ended up his days as a pet, roaming around the yard in front of the house. Another was named Henry, in honor of Henry Dojaquez, a well-known local vaquero, who helped with many round-ups at the ranch.

Jim, Carrie and baby Sam at the Fraizer homestead. 1920.

Chapter Nine

Starting a Family

After four years of marriage, Jim and Carrie sent Samuel the happy news that they were expecting their first baby. Carrie's mother had passed away in February, so she and Jim invited Samuel to come out for a long visit. He arrived on June 14, 1919, and again chronicled his visit in the same hand-written journal in which he had so carefully recorded his first trip. His first entry read, "John and Rhoda met me at the train at 4 p.m. and we went to Carrie's for dinner."

By this time, Esther and Bruce Rothrock had moved to Patagonia. Ironically, Esther came to detest the life that she had described in such glorious terms to her sisters just six years previously. She said that she was either having a baby or just had one. She delivered three babies while she lived in Elgin and couldn't get away fast enough. As soon as they proved up they moved to Patagonia. The Rothrocks retained title to land, but had no desire to come back because as they said, "You had the land but you certainly couldn't eat it." Since they were visiting in Pennsylvania for the summer, John McCarty spent many hours at their homestead, haying for them and repairing fences.

At this time, Jim's brother, Ike Fraizer, was the Arizona State Highway Engineer in charge of new road construction in southeastern Santa Cruz and western Cochise Counties. Knowing of Samuel's avid interest in everything about the area, Ike offered to take him on a grand tour of his projects. They headed to Fairbank, a thriving shipping point on the rail line for the silver mines in Tombstone. "We ate a fine dinner in Fairbank on the State's account," Samuel recorded. They spent the night there before proceeding on to Tombstone and Bisbee to view the progress of the roadwork at those sites. Samuel jotted down specific details of the landscape with his usual enthusiasm. Their return trip took them to Benson, Tucson and finally back to Nogales, where Ike was headquartered.

Three months later, on September 15, 1919, Samuel casually noted in his diary that Carrie had not been feeling well for a few days, and Rhoda had spent the night tending to her. At 11 a.m. that morning she gave birth to her firstborn child, a son Samuel James, named for her father, much to his delight. Samuel recorded that the healthy baby boy weighed in at 8 pounds.

In late October, after an 18-week stay, Samuel reluctantly prepared to leave for home. He described his feelings: "Thus ended my third (he must have come west at some time before Rhoda and Carrie moved to Arizona) and probably my last extended trip to the Far West." Happily, he was actually able to return again the following year, when Sam was about 16 months old.

Carrie, baby Sam, and Samuel. 1920.

During this visit, Samuel made an $800 loan to Jim and Carrie, with an interest rate of six percent per year. The loan was for a term of one year, but when Samuel died in 1922, there was still a balance due. At the time of his death he was 78 years old and had five surviving children who were to share equally in his estate. Carrie received a

Loan document dated, June 1, 1920, in the amount of $800 at six percent interest, payable in one year, to S. J. Swigart. Signed by James G. and Carrie S. Fraizer.

letter from J.C. Swigart, the executor of Samuel's estate, dated January 1, 1923, explaining the distribution Samuel's assets:

Original loan to the Fraizer's	$800.00
Interest due	20.00
Total owed	820.00
Carrie's share of the estate	474.41
Loan from Fraizers to Samuel	175.00
Payment from Fraizer to Samuel	200.00
Total credits	849.41
Balance of Carrie's inheritance	$29.41

Baby Sam perched on the hood of a car with his grandfather Samuel holding him steady. 1920.

Carrie and Jim continued to add to their acreage whenever an opportunity arose and if they could scrape enough cash together. Eventually they increased their holdings to 6,000 acres, including both private and leased land. Ike and Charlie Fraizer had moved to another relinquishment near Elgin sometime after Carrie and Jim were married, and at the beginning of World War I, they bought up both of the brothers' original homesteads. By this time they had a growing cattle operation and Carrie registered her brand with the State Livestock Board.

I Hereby Certify, That the following is a true and correct copy of the entry of the recorded Brand and Mark therein described as the same appears of record in State Brand Book of Arizona 5 in the office of Live Stock Sanitary Board of Arizona, at Phoenix, Arizona, to-wit:

Certificate No. 17226

STATE BRAND BOOK OF ARIZONA
OWNER, POST OFFICE LOCATION OF RANGE

(Page) 2464
PRESENTED FOR RECORD

Hour	Day	Month	Year
9 a.m.	9	Feb.	1916

Carrie S. Fraizer, Elgin, Ariz.

Range: Coronado Nat'l Forest, northern Santa Cruz County, Ariz.

BRANDS OF CATTLE — BRANDS OF HORSES, MULES AND ASSES

LOCATION OF BRAND— left ribs of cattle, left shoulder of horses

Certificate of Secretary

I hereby certify that the Marks and Brands appearing opposite hereto were duly recorded for the said Carrie S. Fraizer at 2 o'clock P. M., on this 7 day of March 1916.

SAM B. BRADNER,
Secretary Live Stock Sanitary Board.

Remarks:

As witness my signature and the seal of the Live Stock Sanitary Board hereunto affixed at Phoenix, Arizona, this 7 day of March 1916.

Secretary of Live Stock Sanitary Board.

Carrie's brand the Lazy 7 Slash 7 was registered March 7, 1916.

Carrie shows her new baby, Jean, the cows in their pasture. 1922.

Their family grew again in 1922 with the birth of their daughter Jean. Sam and Jean were typical ranch children of that era. As Carrie explained, "I don't suppose we ever had more than 150 cows, but my husband didn't like the cattle business, so my children, before they were old enough to go to school, helped pull a calf." They also collected eggs from the chickens, planted crops and spent hours hammering nails to straighten them for yet another of Jim's building projects. Most of all, they enjoyed the outdoors, riding their donkey and when they were old enough, horses, to explore all the surrounding countryside. They attended the one-room school in Elgin and at one time their neighbor, Cora Everhart, was their teacher. Both the children graduated from Patagonia High School, where Sam was a star on the football team.

Carrie, with Sam sitting on the hood of their Model T Ford, and Jean. It was their first car and cost them $650. Carrie said she finally learned to crank it when Jim was laid up in the hospital with a burst appendix. Ca. 1923.

Jean and Sam Fraizer on their donkey. Ca. 1924.

Sam and Jean Fraizer on horseback. Ca. 1928.

Sam and Jean Fraizer with their parents Jim and Carrie, their dog and some of their many cats.

Jim Fraizer, dubbed the Mayor of Elgin, played the role of a trapper in the John Wayne classic, Red River, nominated for an Academy Award in 1948.

Chapter Ten

Community Spirit

"Do you have a movie star in your own back yard?" This was the question posed to readers of the October 22, 1946 issue of the Nogales Daily Herald, as the story went on to describe the part Jim Fraizer was playing in the Howard Hawks' epic movie, Red River. The article continued, "Big Jim Fraizer, commonly known as the Mayor of Elgin, has been assigned a part in the $3 million production. Fraizer has blossomed out in a beard and will play a role as a trapper in the scene where 3,000 cattle are driven over the old Chisholm Trail to the frontier town of Abilene, Kansas.

"On his first appearance before the clicking cameras, Fraizer got tangled up with the sound equipment and his big voice boomed all over the lot, causing a flurry among the directors who rushed in and stopped the action. The Mayor of Elgin, so movie people say, is an ideal character part in the production. All he had to do was grow whiskers and move into the picture. His wife has also been assigned a part. Several other ranchers in the area are taking parts as extras as well as a number of locals, but Fraizer is topping the list in his bid for movie fame."

Jean, Jim and Ilene Fraizer all had parts as extras in Red River.

Red River crew filming the cattle drive headed toward the Biscuit in the Mustang Mountains in Elgin. (Al Sisk photo from the Nogales Herald, October 22, 1946.)

John Wayne "takes five" to relax during the filming of Red River with members of the Boice family, owners of the historic Empire Ranch near Sonoita, where the movie was filmed. With Wayne, from left, are Frank "Pancho" Boice, Bob Boice, and their mother, Mary Boice.
(Photo courtesy the Boice family and the Empire Ranch Foundation.)

Howard Hawks wasn't the only one in the area who could put on an extravagant theatrical production however. Kit Hutchinson who owned and operated the Little Outfit Ranch School in the San Rafael Valley along with her husband, Buell, had an enduring passion for drama and put on many school plays that the residents from miles around flocked to attend. She was such an inspiring figure that the male students even agreed to play the part of girls just to keep the scenes moving.

The Elgin Community Players

present their

Folly '53

"Good Afternoon! Ritz Hotel"

Saturday, April 25 – 8:30
ELGIN COMMUNITY CLUB

Thursday, April 30 – Friday, May 1 – 8:30
STAR THEATRE, NOGALES

Playbill for "Good Afternoon Ritz Hotel," one of Elgin Club's most ambitious productions.

CAST

(In Order Of Appearance)

Manager	"Bum" Hedgcock
Stella, Telephone Girl	Sherry Boice
Miss Beebe, "Bounteous Bertha"	Marianne Creamer
Bellhops	Bob Grennan, Frank Hedgcock, Russel Van Gorder, Larry Burgess
Char-ladies	Carrie Fraizer, Mary Burgess, Ruth Anderson, Esther Schock
Ralph	Wagner Schorr
Susie	Marie Schorr
Daphne	Jane Holbrook
Playboy	Brainard Douglas
Babe	Fay Collie
Mac	Regean Gardner
Julia	Patricia Burton
Mildred	Sally Grennan
Dot	Elene Fraizer
Percy Pennyfeather	Joe Creamer
Mr. Mangodiavanci	Sam Fraizer
Harold Banner	Frank Burton
Mattie Banner	Cora Babcock
'Jam'	Ray Schock
Clyde Warren	Stone Collie
Bessie Warren	Mary Boice
John	Ned Hutchinson
Mrs. Needringheimenbusher	Hettie Lee Gardner
Mrs. Fish	Frances Hedgcock
Mr. Fish	'Pancho' Boice
Mr. Needringheimenbusher	Walter Kolbe
Traveling Man	Jim Fraizer
Bride	Della Southers
Groom	Leroy Southers
Waitresses	Judy Grennan, Donna White, Marilyn Parker, Charlsie Byrd, Nancy Grennan
Head Waiter	Frank Hedgcock
Princess Maui Lani	Mary Harris
Queen Kalakaua	Fay Hill
Hortense	Kit Hutchinson
The Ritz Tomatoes	Sally Grennan, Jane Holbrook, Gladys White
Understudies	Jay Fierst, Bill Anderson

Cast of Characters for "Good Afternoon Ritz Hotel."

After selling the ranch, the Hutchinsons moved to the Sonoita area in the 1950s and Kit continued writing and directing plays and musicals, this time at the Elgin Community Club. The entire Fraizer family, along with dozens of other club members, acted in many of these. One of the most memorable was Folly '53, "Good Afternoon Ritz Hotel," which was presented at both the Elgin Community Club and at the Star Theatre in Nogales, through the auspices of the Nogales Little Theater.

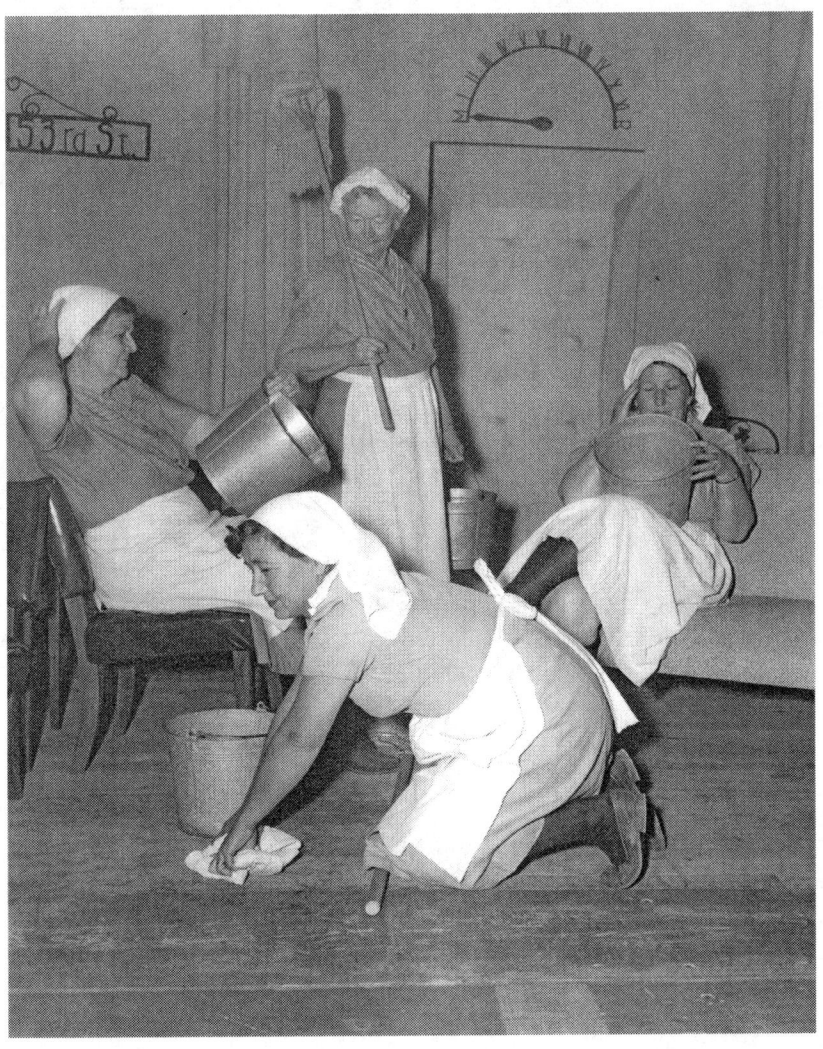

The char-ladies at the Ritz Hotel. Carrie Fraizer standing, Esther Schock and Ruth Anderson seated, Mary Burgess scrubbing the floor.

Cast of "Good Afternoon Ritz Hotel." Carrie Fraizer can be seen at the far right in the third row. The waitresses in the front row from left: Judy Grennan, Donna White, Marilyn Parker and Nancy Grennan. The "Ritz Tomatoes" in the second row: Sally Grennan, Jane Holbrook and Gladys White. 1953.

The Elgin Club was formed in 1932, according to charter member Marka Moss, when a man named Mr. Ramsey donated land on which to build the clubhouse. Marka's father, Stone Collie, built the fireplace using rocks from his nearby property. The main room included a large stage that was perfect for theatrical productions. Children used to roller skate on the wood floors until the resulting damage caused a halt to that activity. Originally a women's club, men were invited to join starting in 1949.

An annual party was held February 22 to celebrate Washington's Birthday, at that time a national holiday, now combined with Lincoln's birthday and known as Presidents Day. The women handmade all the costumes and couples danced the Virginia reel, the Minuet, and other old time favorites. In December, the Elgin School put on their annual Christmas play there.

The George Washington's Birthday party at the Elgin Club. From left, Sam Fraizer, Carrie, Jean, John McCarty and Rhoda McCarty.

A group of Elgin School students put on a Christmas play blending Hispanic and Anglo cultures in 1958. The pageant was held on the large stage at the Elgin Community Club. Students include at left Junior Dojaquez, and Tom Piper. Fourth from right is Smokey Ambrose. (Photo courtesy of Posy Piper.)

Ida Turney of Rain Valley suggested forming an Elgin Book Circle to give women from far-flung ranches a chance to get together, dress up as proper ladies and discuss interesting books. The group was limited to 17 members who met twice a year; once in January to elect officers and choose the books for the year, and again in March for a social meeting where they dressed up in hat and gloves and discussed the books. Each member purchased one book, had two weeks to read it, and then passed it on to the next person on the list, ensuring that each one would read all 17 books by the end of the year.

Carrie Fraizer and Fern Collie, Marka's mother, were among the first members. The women were not called by their first names, referring to each other as Mrs.

When Alfred Henry Lewis's "Wolfville," was first published in 1897, Theodore Roosevelt had not yet become President, and the West was still the "Old West." Lewis, himself a Westerner, immediately became the most popular of the Western writers of the day and his Old Cattleman, Doc Peets and Faro Nell became household words. These characters still resonated 35 years later, as testified by the reception of "Wolfville," when it was republished for the 14th time by Frederick A. Stokes Company. This book, one of the club's first selections, was suggested by Rhoda McCarty.

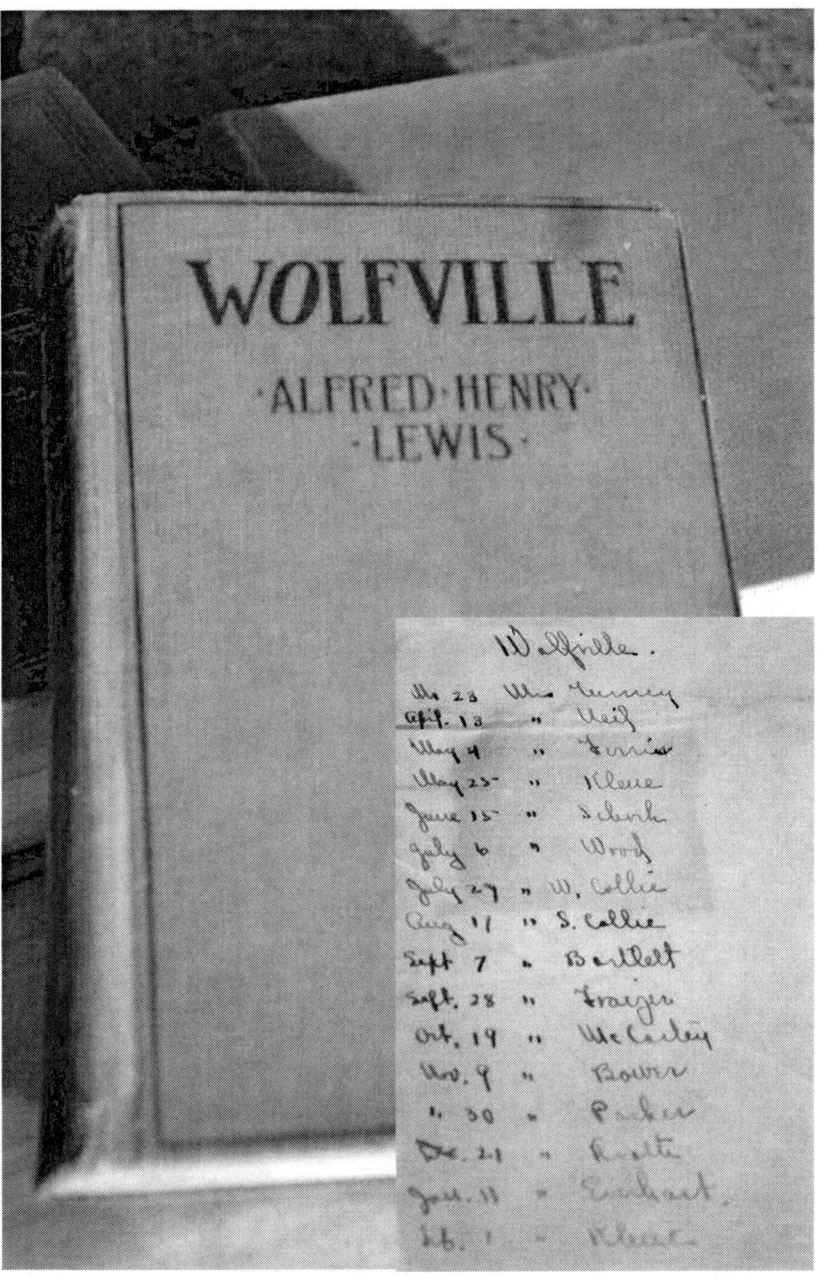

This handwritten note is still taped inside the book. It lists each member and the date she is to read the book, along with the date and name of the member who is to read it next. The members were Mrs. Turney, Neil, Ferris, Klene, Schock, Wood, Wm. Collie, Stone Collie, Bartlett, Fraizer, McCarty, Bower, Parker, Roath, and Everhart. (Cheryl Rogos photos.)

Bartlett, Mrs. Roath and so on. Carrie collected all the books at the end of each year and kept the collection in a special bookcase in her living room.

Although Carrie had been a devoted member of the Elgin Club for 30 years, hurt feelings seemed to cause her to resign her membership, at least temporarily. In a letter to her daughter Jean written July 6, 1962, she said, "I have really been upset over the actions of the club and I am now out of it for good. Maybe it's for the best. It has made quite a stir as all the old members have made a fuss. I am sorry too, because I blame Jerry (sic) the most of all. (Gerry Van Gorder's husband owned the Elgin Store.) She holds the mortgage on the Clubhouse and has her finger in everything. She has acted so much as though she was my friend. If there was a bunch it wouldn't be so bad, but it's only me."

Elgin Club Book Circle in 1971. First row, from left: Marstelle Cornwall, Betty Bunnell, Carrie Fraizer, Minnie Kunde, Fern Collie, Sally Grennan. Second row: Cassie Mellor, Beth Smith, Gerry Van Gorder, Kay Lowy, Marka Moss, Deanna Sims, Joan Hedgcock. (Photo courtesy of the Elgin Community Club archives.)

The Elgin Store, operated by Russell and Gerry Van Gorder, also housed the Post Office and was a favorite gathering grounds for the locals. This post card dubs Elgin as a place where the sun shines and the wind blows. (Courtesy Bowman and Stradling History Center.)

This bump in the road blew over eventually, and a 1971 issue of the Nogales International, accompanied by a photo of Carrie and Pat Basinger, Elgin Club Secretary, touts the work of the group in making the Sonoita Rodeo a success. It reported, "The group of people who make up the staunch Elgin Community Club are one very large reason why the annual rodeo is always a winner...the Community Club works almost year round toward a successful rodeo and fair.

Taking charge of concessions and refreshments, its members make sure that hungry cowboys and their audiences are well fed and watered (loosely speaking) at every gathering"

Roscoe Babcock acted as chief chef in 1955 when a group of Elgin Club women dished up meals during the Sonoita Horse Races at the Fairgrounds. With him from left: Hettie Lee Gardner, Marie Schorr, Faye Hill, Mary Bowman, Ella Braden, Jane Williams, Lou Schock and Kit Hutchinson. Their sign read: Hot dogs .25, Cake .15, Pie .20. (Photo courtesy Bowman and Stradling History Center.)

The Santa Cruz County Cowbelles held many renowned "Cowbelle picnics" in Canelo at the historic cienega on the William "Billy" Parker ranch. Carrie Fraizer is pictured at the bottom of the photo, far left. The site is now owned by Parker's grandson, Byrd Lindsey. (Photo courtesy Cowbelles Ranchers' Heritage Center).

Carrie became charter member of the Santa Cruz County Cowbelles, formed in August 1947. Of the women present at a meeting at the Patagonia Women's Club to hear Mrs. Ralph Cowan, President of the Arizona State Cowbelles, 32 decided to form a county group to be known as the Santa Cruz County Cowbelles. They immediately became the nucleus of Charter Members. Their stated purpose was to contribute to the growth and development of the cattle industry and to promote friendship and respect among the members of the cattle ranching community. Carrie was a devoted member of the group for the rest of her life.

This undated formal photo of Carrie Fraizer was taken at an Arizona Cattlemen's Convention in Phoenix. (Photo courtesy of Cowbelles Ranchers' Heritage Center.)

In addition to her many community activities, Carrie loved to travel. Whether it was around the state with her local girlfriends or out of the country with her family, she was always eager to explore new vistas. One such trip was planned by Laura Bergier whose family ranched in the Patagonia area. In another letter to her daughter Jean, this one dated in the Spring of 1960, she writes, "Laura planned a driving trip to Northern Arizona with me, Leota Gatlin and another woman who had to cancel, so she invited Edna. "I think I would just as soon stay home. She is so sarcastic lately. Maybe I will tell her off in a nice way before we get back. When I have enough I have enough."

The Edna she referred to was Edna Houston, a close neighbor and "sometimes" close friend. They had many blow-ups over the years, as evidenced by Edna's instructions to her grandchildren in the event of her death. "My grandmother told us, 'Do not put my birth date on the tombstone. I don't want Carrie Fraizer looking over and knowing how old I am,'" Barbara Bowers Jones said. This, in spite of the fact that Carrie was already dead and buried in a nearby plot at the Black Oak Pioneer Cemetery.

Edna Houston sits at a campfire in Box Canyon north of Sonoita with her saddle on the ground next to her. A self-taught naturalist, she spent many hours identifying plants and often took her grandchildren, Barbara and Jim Bowers and Bill and David Telles, outside at night to learn about the constellations. (Courtesy of Barbara Bowers Jones.)

Both women were widowed, both strong women running cattle ranches, and both had homesteaded as single women in their youth. Edna had filed on a homestead in Kansas but lost the property because another settler reported that she did not live on it full time. Edna and Carrie belonged to all the same community organizations and went on many trips together. Despite all they had in common, or possibly because of it, there was a rivalry between the two that seemed to continue beyond the grave.

Carrie took a trip to Mexico with her family in 1954 when she was about 73 years old. From left: Sam, Jean, Mexican tour guide, Carrie and Ilene enjoy a river cruise.

Carrie had no hesitation in accepting invitations from her son Sam and his wife Ilene however. As she wrote to Jean another time, "Sam says they have been talking about a trip for some time but just now told me. Leave on Friday for San Diego, spend Saturday and Sunday there and return Monday. Asked if I would like to come along – 'Foolish question!' Dave, one of his (Sam's) men, lives at

Everharts' and he can stop by and feed the cats and dogs. Grace (an ailing mother cow) will have to manage."

Carrie Fraizer's Hereford cattle graze on the range at her homestead. The Mustang Mountains rise in the background. (Ray Manley photo from the family's collection.)

Chapter Eleven
Alone Again

The late spring morning in 1955 started out peacefully at the Fraizer homestead. Carrie had gone out running errands and Jim was eager to get to a painting job out in the barn. He worked a few hours and when he was ready to take a break, he cleaned up the equipment with gasoline and unthinkingly stuffed the cleaning rag in his pocket. Then he rolled a cigarette and lit a match.

The resulting fire burned down the barn and Jim was badly hurt, but able to crawl outside.

No one was around at the time and he lay there for several hours before someone finally found him. In a cruel twist of fate, Jim would be mortally injured in a fiery explosion, as his brother Ike had been, many years previously. About six months later, having never recovered from his injuries, Jim Fraizer died in a Phoenix hospital, December 17, 1955. He and Carrie had been married for forty years.

Once again, Carrie found herself alone on the land. Even though Jim had not liked the cattle business and was rarely seen on a horse, he had more than pulled his weight, performing all the mechanical and construction duties and the myriad other tasks that come with running an outfit in a remote area, as well as holding down a job at Ft. Huachuca. Now it would all be up to Carrie.

Fortunately her son Sam lived nearby in Sonoita, where he ran a successful garage and his wife, Ilene, owned the local Café. Sam, along with Bill Piper, Jokie Spencer, and Henry Dojaquez helped her with roundups and doctoring, but

Sam Fraizer owned a garage and Texaco service station near the Sonoita Crossroads. (Photo courtesy Ilene Fraizer.)

the day-to-day was up to Carrie.

She met the challenge with her usual determination and can-do attitude. However, several years later Carrie became uncharacteristically discouraged as evidenced by this letter to her daughter Jean, who by that time was married and living in Phoenix:

"Dear Jean, All bad news. I don't know that I ever came nearer breaking. I wonder if these storms will ever end. The car has never moved since Fred (Jean's husband Fred Rowley) put it there, and no telling when it will. Sam comes every couple of days and feeds the cattle hay. Half a ton a day, but there is simply nothing for them to eat and we have 20 little calves. They have all lived so far as we know, but Friday he couldn't get through Hiltons' (a nearby pasture) even in the pickup with chains. Wasn't able to get in the south pasture at all. He may ride the horse today when he comes, if we can't get through.

"I am just about out of wood and it's all wet and covered with snow. The oil line leaks on the porch so bad it nearly all leaked away and I can't burn it. I don't know what I would do without the electric heaters. I am never warm except in bed. This is another record as it was two degrees below zero this morning and has been six and seven above all week.

Carrie, probably on her way back from Sunday services, hand-feeds one of the new calves near her corral.

One of the mother cows, probably Grace, who was a dependable producer for many years.

"Old Grace (one of her favorite mother cows) just about drove me crazy. She never gets any better but can still get up. Her calf will be four weeks old Wednesday, and if she dies I don't know how to raise it, as I can't even get out for any milk. Last Friday she went out a few steps into the corral into a foot of mush and went down and I couldn't get her up. I covered her with a blanket as it was starting to snow again.

"I didn't sleep all night and expected to find her dead in the morning but there she was in the barn. The bone was broken that goes from her backbone to her hip. Think of the vitality she has at 13 years old. She is still helping out with Priscilla's calf which so near died at New Years. It can go out with its mother when the weather gets better."

Somehow, Carrie survived this crisis, and by October she was thrilled and proud to win the Reserved Champion in the lightweight category for her pen of three steers at the Santa Cruz County Fair. She referred to the award as her "Oscar," and was especially pleased because there were 22 pens full of competitors. Bill Piper was the judge and found hers the most uniform according to Carrie's records, averaging 407 pounds and bringing .40 cents per pound. At a recognition ceremony at the Patagonia Woman's Club, it was said that few if any cattlemen in the State can equal her calf-crop record, her percentage being in the high 90s.

Austin Moss working cattle on the Rose Tree Ranch, in Elgin. He and his wife, Marka, lived nearby on the Mustang Ranch, which originally belonged to her parents, Fern and Stone Collie. The Biscuit is seen in the background. (Courtesy Marka Moss.)

A year or two later, Carrie went over to Harold Tovrea's Swinging H Ranch, managed by Austin Moss, to talk to him about buying a bull. Carrie noticed that his wife, Marka, was pregnant with her fourth or fifth child, and made some comment about it to Austin. He told her, "Mrs. Fraizer, when I took over at Swinging H, Mr. Tovrea told me he wanted a 100 per cent calf crop. I'm just doing my part."

Some of Carrie's horses. She rode the range until about age 80, when she switched to driving her old Dodge Dart over the pastures. She had a perimeter road up on the ridge and if a cow was down she could usually spot it from the car.

Henry Dojaquez said Carrie was a good horsewoman and he especially remembered Frances, a beautiful palomino who went out to pasture when Carrie quit riding at age 80. When Carrie decided she was too old to ride, Henry used to kid her. He said, "When are you going to retire your horse, what retirement does she get?" One time, Henry went to help out at Fraizer's, and just as he got there, he said, "Carrie was in the corral and a calf knocked her down. The front of her legs was (sic) all bruised and I picked her up (the calf) and put her in the corner. Well, the calf was spooky you know. I don't know if I hadn't been there what the calf would have done." Carrie was hurt, but she doctored herself up and they continued with the sorting.

Henry Dojaquez, well-known local vaquero who helped Carrie and son Sam with many roundups. Dojaquez credits his cattle savvy to watching and learning from his father, Miguel, who came to the U.S. in 1907 to work on the railroad. Miguel had had experience with the Greene Cattle Company in Mexico and later worked at big local ranches including the Empire, Douglas and Boquillas. His mother Felicita Escalante arrived in 1905 with her parents. Her father worked at the Helvetia Mines. (Photo courtesy Bowman and Stradling History Center.)

Henry continued, "She could go in the pasture and she knew them (sic) cows and she could walk up to them. A stranger, no, but she could. She had them marked when she weaned them. The heifers she wanted to keep. I remember the first time I was helping Sam and she wanted to look at a certain cow and Sam was busy getting ready to ship.

"She said, Sam there's a cow – her name is ___ she's got a spot here and a spot there. Well, Sam rode and rode and finally said, 'Henry see if you can find her.' Mrs. Fraizer said – I'll never forget – she said, it's got a wide red spot under her jaw here. I said, okay. I went slow, looked at the calves, finally I spotted her. So I brought the calf where she could see it, and Carrie said that's the cow. She wanted to see the heifer because she wanted to keep it. She said yep, I like the heifer, so I cut her out."

Grandson, Jim Rowley, told of the time she had a sick calf in the corral. "Carrie was small, but the first thing she did was reach down in its throat and see if there was a blockage there. The next day it started running around in circles and went down. It was rabid, so she had to get a series of rabies shots every day. She had to drive to the Texaco Station at the Crossroads where her son Sam had his station, to meet the doctor, or maybe a vet, I'm not sure. The calf probably got bitten by a skunk, but the calf didn't bite her. The shots were just a precaution."

Carrie's hobby, and her driving passion next to cows and cats, was collecting glass bottles from various landfills around the county. She went on many bottle hunting excursions with her friend Kay Lowy from Canelo, who always seemed to be able to locate new dumps to explore. What they were looking for especially were the bottles that were made during the depression era and turned a purple color after being exposed to the sun for a period of time. Her collection also included other colors such as brown, blue and green, all of which she spent hours scrubbing to get off the paint and dirt. She sorted them and kept careful count of each, listed separately by their color.

Her goal was to get to 2,000 bottles, a goal she more than surpassed over the next 15 years. Carrie told an interviewer, "I had 10,000 and my garage burned down. There were about 3,000 in there, which (sic) they all melted up. I must have 9,000 now. They are not what I call valuable. It isn't money I'm looking for, it's pleasure."

Evidently Carrie was not the only one interested in collecting bottles. She told her daughter, "I know where a person can get enough brown beer bottles to build a house if they were desired, (they are located) below the old Canelo store.

Carrie in her living room with a small portion of her huge bottle collection. Ca. late 1960s.

Hank Isaacs has one I would give my eyeteeth for but I couldn't talk him out of it. He had saved me some other ones though."

In, 1960, Carrie again wrote to Jean, "There was the most awful wind came just before it rained. The front door was open and before I could get it shut it even blew the framed pictures off the wall by the stove. Blew the roof off the gas house and the north side of the carpenter shop. The roof didn't do any damage as it landed up the hill by the fence. But oh the shambles in my bottles.

"There was a window frame, several table legs, the long timbers with the clamps of a gun barrel tumbled down in my bottles. I suppose I will never know how many were broken. Mostly brown ones. A lot were knocked on the ground and weren't broken. It could have been worse but it's bad enough. Maybe Charles (probably Charles Putnam who had moved back from Oregon with his new wife and was working for Sam) and Sam will try to put it back on the carpenter shop."

Whenever Jean and the children came to visit, dumpster diving was on the menu. Jim Rowley remembers the time they were at a landfill south of Patagonia and he and Carrie hurried out of the car and had already started searching when he heard his mom calling them. He said, "Janet got her leg cut. She fell as soon as she got out of the car, gashed her leg real bad and it was bleeding a lot. We ran down to Dr. Mock's and he got the blood stopped. She still has a scar on her knee. That's the only time anyone got hurt on those expeditions. Dr. Mock was retired, so he was home!" Delmar Mock, M.D. was a true "country doctor" who made house calls across the county and even treated animals when no vet was available.

Jean and the kids, Jim and Janet, also liked to camp out when they visited Carrie. One time they brought two dogs with them and the dogs got too close to the javelina that were feeding nearby. Carrie said, "The dogs ran to the family for protection and the pigs followed them.

This purple bottle, one of the most beautiful in her collection, is now owned by her grandson, Jim Rowley. It is a prime example of the process wherein the glass, which contains manganese, turns a shade of very light to medium purple after several years of exposure to the rays of the sun. This was frequently termed "SCA" (sun-colored-amethyst) or "desert glass" by bottle collectors especially in the 1960s and 1970s. (Cheryl Rogos photo).

And they all got up a tree. The one dog got up the tree but the other dog couldn't make it. So Jim had to get down in front of the hogs and rescue the little dog to get it up the tree. They were up there about two hours. The old sow stayed until finally she took a notion to go home."

Carrie was at the depot to see the last train to come through Elgin in 1962 almost 50 years after she had arrived at the same stop in 1913. From left: Jim, Janet and Jean Rowley, Lynn Fraizer and Carrie. (Ilene Fraizer Photo, courtesy Lynn Kelley.)

Chapter Twelve
The Legacy Endures

"The railroad was everything. No one could have gotten here without the railroad. It meant life to everybody. There were no roads." Carrie uttered these words to an interviewer many years after she arrived on the Southern Pacific Railroad in 1913. The depot served as a post office and shipping point for the local mines and cattle ranches, and the trainmen's arrivals were eagerly anticipated for they not only delivered packages and mail, but also brought welcome world and national news to a rural area basically cut off from the rest of the country. One can only imagine her emotions as she and her daughter and three of her grandchildren watched the last train to ever pull out of that very same depot, 49 years later.

The ensuing ten years were to bring many more changes to Carrie's life. She was getting older and it was becoming more difficult with each passing year to continue with all her many ranching and community commitments. She always stepped up when she perceived a need, however, and when the town of Patagonia decided to enhance the town park, Carrie was among the first to donate a beautiful tree, dedicated in honor of Jim Fraizer. A road named Fraizer Drive in Sonoita also honors this well-loved member of the community.

In 1946 Carrie lost her dear sister and lifelong close companion, Rhoda, who had lived almost 35 years on the adjoining homestead. Although not as active in the community as Carrie, she and John were devoted members of the nearby Vaughn Church. After her passing, John later remarried and moved to Patagonia. They had no children.

Easter Sunday services at the Vaughn Church, 1936. Seated: Emory Stoddard, Mr. Speed, Mr. Geiger, Annie Black, Rhoda McCarty, Mrs. and Mr. Buck, Della Honnas, Fred Putnam, Virginia and Charlie Gardner. Standing: Ed LeGendre, John McCarty, John White, Mrs. and Mr. Benjamin, Charlie Putnam, Dorothy Putnam. (Courtesy Bowman and Stradling History Center.)

Her sister Esther and her husband, Bruce Rothrock, moved to Salem, Oregon in the 1920s, where many of their relatives and neighbors had relocated. Although she kept in constant touch, she was quite far away and Carrie and Rhoda missed her greatly. Their son, Oliver, named for his grandfather, remained in the area for the rest of his life, serving as Justice of the Peace in Patagonia as well as driving the school bus and maintaining the grounds at the Patagonia High School. He would stay at Carrie's during the week, to make it more convenient to pick up

Oliver Rothrock holding a rifle at the gas station in Patagonia owned by Buck Blabon in 1937. Oliver was the son of Bruce and Esther and the namesake of Bruce's father. He lost his leg in an auto accident at a young age and made himself a wooden one that he strapped to his waist, concealed under his clothes. "Old axe handles make the best legs," he claimed. For dress occasions, he wore a regulation artificial leg. When Joker Mendoza lost his leg in a mining accident, Oliver appeared at his door with an axe handle, offering to make one for him. (Courtesy Bill Bergier.)

and drop off the Elgin and Sonoita area children. On weekends he would return to his own home in Patagonia.

Carrie's interest in everything going on in the community around her remained steadfast throughout the years. Her granddaughter, Lynn Fraizer Kelley, remembered how Carrie loved the Fourth of July celebration in Nogales. She always took Sam's family with her to watch the fireworks from their special vantage point. They had a standing invitation from Jim's brother, Charlie Fraizer and his wife, Emma Mae, to watch from their home on the hill overlooking the old Nogales High School. At Christmastime, Sam and family would take her in to Tucson to drive through the Festival of Lights in the Winterhaven subdivision, and enjoy the beautifully decorated houses all lit up for the season.

Lynn and her grandmother were quite close and when Lynn got the urge to see her, she would jump on her bike without telling anyone and pedal the ten miles or so to the homestead. After a long visit, Carrie would roll the bike up in the back of the car and drive the little 12-year old back to Sonoita.

Carrie was infamous for driving her car anywhere, on whatever kind of surface, from paved road to rocky pasture. Jim Rowley remembers scary rides where Carrie would "take a piece right out of the middle of the road. And she'd go hell-bent-for-Sunday over all those dips and stuff. If she hit a rock she'd say it wasn't there before, and she knew where everything was, pretty much. Many times she tore up the underside of that car hitting rocks and things.

"She kept the hay in the trunk of the car. She'd have Sam or someone put a bale in there for her, then she'd go out and feed the cows. She had an old Dodge Dart, for riding the range, and a Chrysler that was her going-to-town car. The Dodge was an old style that you started with a push button. It was a '62 I think. The buttons were on the dashboard. There was a lever you threw to put it out of park, and the gears were push buttons. That's the car I learned to drive in."

Arizona Cattlewoman

In 1956 there was a festive 75th birthday party for Carrie at the Elgin Club. One of her friends, Cora Babcock, wrote this poem to honor her:

"Tribute to Carrie"

Here's to you Carrie, a Gay Nineties Girl...
You came out West to give it a whirl.
You took up some land, a home you made.
In true western style, you made the grade.
A single "miss" you didn't remain
"Jim" came along and changed your name...
As time passed by, you raised some cattle;
You learned to ride and rope from the saddle.
You could build a fence or doctor a cow

Whatever it was, you knew "how"
We love you, Carrie, for the things you have done
You helped build this Club House
Where we gather for fun.
Many things I could write, only mentioned a few.
With true pioneer spirit you've served us well
We gather here to tell you, we think you're SWELL
"Many Happy Returns" on your 75th Day
God Bless and keep you, is our wish today.

One of Carrie's many birthday parties, probably her 85th. Front row, from left: Lynn Fraizer, Janet and Jim Rowley, Ross Fraizer. Back row: Jean Fraizer Rowley, Carrie, Sam and Ilene Fraizer.

Possibly the greatest tribute that her son, Sam, could give to his mother was continuing her example of giving back to the community. Sam Fraizer was deeply involved in the Santa Cruz County Fair and Rodeo Association, serving as president in 1957, during which time he installed the electricity for the pump and performed the maintenance on the pump and the well.

Two female firefighters give Sam Fraizer a farewell kiss at his 1979 retirement party after 23 years as the volunteer fire chief in Sonoita. He and his successor, Jokie Spencer, turned the first shovels of dirt when rancher Bettie Ann Beck donated land for a permanent fire department in 1989. (Courtesy Sonoita Elgin Fire District.)

Sam was the first to recognize the need for fire protection for the community and organized the Sonoita/Elgin Fire Association in 1956. He assessed members a fee to raise money which enabled them to purchase a surplus 1941 Chevrolet fire truck from Fort Huachuca, and served as Sonoita Elgin fire chief for 23 years.

Her grandson, Jim Rowley, an electrical contractor, is past president of the Elgin Club and serves on the board of the Fair & Rodeo Association, continuing to keep the Fraizer tradition alive in the community. Jim's sister, Janet Thompson, is soon to move to the area and has already begun community service as well.

On Carrie's 90th birthday the family hosted a huge gala at Pioneer Hall at the Fairgrounds in Sonoita, where 200 guests gathered to celebrate with her. Messages were received from Sen. Barry Goldwater, Congressman Morris Udall and Gov. Jack Williams. Even President Richard Nixon sent congratulations.

Several years later, on Christmas Eve in 1973, Carrie Fraizer passed away. Wade Cavanaugh of the Arizona Daily Star, wrote these words under the headline, "Sonoita Mourns Carrie Fraizer. Carrie was laid to rest at Black Oak Pioneer Cemetery, preserved for those pioneers of the area, next to her husband, Jim. Her request made a long time ago: "This land has been good to me, I never want to leave it."

Simple stones mark the spot where Carrie and Jim Fraizer were both laid to rest at the Black Oak Pioneer Cemetery in Elgin. (Cheryl Rogos photo).

Bibliography

Arizona Daily Star, Associated Press, Miami, Arizona. "Fraizer's Body Recovered From Fire Ruins, Former Nogalian Had Been State, County, and City Engineer." September 17, 1932.

_____, Wade Cavanaugh. "Aged Carrie Fraizer Runs the Ranch," July 11, 1971.

_____, Wade Cavanaugh. "Sonoita Mourns Carrie Fraizer," December 29, 1973.

Arizona Republic, Alma Ready. "Ranchers' Wives Observe 49th Year of Elgin Book Club," 1971.

Barnes, Will C. "Arizona Place Names," The University of Arizona Press. Third printing. 1977.

Brophy, Frank Cullen. "San Ignacio Del Babacomari," Arizona Highways, September, 1966, Reprinted, April, 1917.

Eppinga, Jane. "Nogales, Life and Times on the Frontier," Pimeria Alta Historical Society, Arcadia Press, 2002.

Fraizer, Carrie. Notes for a radio broadcast at Station KNOG, Nogales, Arizona, undated.

Letters from J.C. Swigart, Executor of Estate of Samuel J. Swigart, to Carrie Fraizer, 1923.

Letters to and from Jean Fraizer Rowley and her mother, Carrie Fraizer, 1948.

_____, January, 1960 - June, 1962.

Mendoza, José (Joker). "Back in Them Days – When Patagonia Was a Mining Town," Writers' Club Press, an Imprint of iUniverse, Inc., 2001.

Nogales Daily Herald, no by-line. "Howard Hawks is Filming 'Red River,' an Early-day Western Cattle Story," October 22, 1946.

_____, obituary. "Fraizer Rites Tomorrow at Elgin," December 20, 1955.

_____, no by-line. "Pioneer Woman to Speak Here," November 16, 1968.

Nogales International, no by-line. "Mrs. Carrie Fraizer, Elgin Pioneer, Addresses Woman's Club," November 22, 1968.

_____, photo. "Junior Woman's Club Models," May 2, 1972.

_____, no by-line. "Small Town; Big Contribution, Elgin Group Aids Rodeo, Fair," September 1, 1972.

_____, no by-line. "Carrie Fraizer, an Arizona Pioneer," January 2, 1974.

Piper, Posy; Bowman, Bob. "A History of the Santa Cruz County Fair and Rodeo Association, 1915 – 1965

Ready, Alma. "Open Range and Hidden Silver," Pimeria Alta Historical Society, Alto Press, 1973.

Suagee, Kathy and the San Pedro Valley Arts and Historical Society, "Around Benson," Arcadia Publishing. 2009.

Swigart, Samuel James. Handwritten journal. Trip to Elgin, Arizona, July 14, - August 31, 1914.

_____, Handwritten journal. Trip to Elgin, Arizona, June 14 – October 20, 1919.

The Sentinel, Lewistown, Pennsylvania, Ben Meyers. "Widow Rancher Rides Her Ranch Alone," July 1, 1967.

_____, Hattie Meyers. "Former Lewistowner, Now 90, Is Cow Rancher in Arizona," September 30, 1971.

Whetzel, Mary Wiley. "Echoes Down the Centuries, Memories From the Patagonias and the Sonoita Creek Valley," iUniverse, Inc., 2007.

Wilson, Hattie. "Patagonia: The Way It Was," Dawes Publishing, 2005.

Interviews

Dojaquez, Henry. Interview by author, Sonoita, Arizona, February 4, 2016.

Fraizer, Carrie. Interview by a representative of Pimeria Alta Historical Society, March 6, 1972.

_____, Interview by F. Shoppe of Willcox, Arizona, for the Arizona Historical Society, 1972.

Fraizer, Ilene. Interview by author, Sonoita, Arizona, February 19, 2007.

Kelley, Lynn Fraizer. Interview by author, Tucson, Arizona, May 13, 2016.

Moss, Marka. Interview by author, Elgin, Arizona, July 17, 2016.

Thompson, Janet Rowley. Interview by author, Tucson, Arizona, June 3, 2016

Rowley, Jim. Interview by author, Elgin, Arizona July 29, 2016.

Arizona Cattlewoman

Index

A

Abilene 75
Academy Award 74
Ambrose, Smokey 84
American Museum of Natural History 47
Anderson, Ruth 81
Arizona Daily Star 113
Arizona Territory 56, 60
Ashburn, Oscar 62
Aycock, Nora Beth (Smith) 63, 86

B

Babacomari Land Grant 21
Babcock, Cora 110
Babcock, Roscoe 88
Baldy 18
Barnett, Eva "Ma" 28
Barnett, Harry 30
Bartlett, Marcus 55
Bartlett, Nellie 55, 84
Basinger, Pat 88
Beck, Bettie Ann 112
Beebe 13
Belle of Elgin 28
Benjamin, Mrs. and Mr. 108
Benson 35, 66
Bergier, Bill 108
Bergier, Laura 91
Bisbee 60
Biscuit 48, 77, 99
Blabon, Buck 108
Black, Annie 108
Black Oak Pioneer Cemetery 91, 113
Boice, Bob 78
Boice, Frank "Pancho" 78
Boice, Mary 78
Boquillas Ranch 101
Border Patrol 38
Bowers, Barbara 91

Bowers, Jim 91
Bowman, Mary 88
Box Canyon 91
Braden, Ella 88
Buck, Mrs. and Mr. 108
Bunnell, Betty 86
Burden, Joseph 47
Burgess, Mary 81

C

Canelo 56, 89
Canelo store 102
Capron, Rhonda 9
Capron, Tim 9
Carr, Neil 47
Chico, CA 31
Chisholm Trail 75
Chrysler 109
Church of the Brethren 10, 40
Collie, Bill 55
Collie, Chopeta (Bartlett) 55
Collie, Fern 84, 86, 99
Collie, Reuben 55
Collie, Stone 82, 99
Cornwall, Marstelle 86
Coronado, Francisco Vasquez 11
Cowan, Mrs. Ralph 89
Cowbelle picnics 89
Cowbelles Ranchers' Heritage Center 54

D

Dalton, Albern 37, 38
Dalton, Lorena 37, 38
Dodge Dart 109
Dojaquez, Henry 10, 63, 95, 101
Dojaquez, Junior 84
Dojaquez, Miguel, 101
Douglas Ranch 101

E

Edmonds, Franklin Spencer 16
elderberries 46
Elgin 21, 24

Elgin Book Circle 84
Elgin Club 79, 81, 82, 88, 110, 112
Elgin Depot 30
Elgin Hotel 14
Elgin School 84
Elgin Store 86
Elias, Don Ignacio 11
Elias, Doña Eulalia 11
El Paso, TX 62
Empire Ranch 36, 78, 101
Empire Ranch Foundation 14
Escalante, Felicita 101
Estavanico 11
Everhart, Charles 60, 61, 93
Everhart, Cora 60, 61, 70

F

Fairbank, AZ 31, 48, 65
Fort Huachuca 36, 62, 95, 112
Fraizer, Carrie Swigart 4, 12, 13, 15, 16, 20, 24, 26, 29, 30, 31, 34, 36, 38, 41, 43, 45, 46, 51, 52, 55, 60, 62, 64, 66, 67, 70, 82, 83, 84, 86, 91, 102, 111
Fraizer, Charlie 25, 50, 51, 109
Fraizer Drive 107
Fraizer, Emma Mae 109
Fraizer, Ike 25, 51, 65, 68, 95
Fraizer, Ilene 26, 50, 63, 76, 92, 96, 111
Fraizer, Jim 21, 25, 34, 35, 46, 50, 51, 53, 55, 58, 60, 62, 64, 67, 76, 95, 107
Fraizer, Ross 111
Fraizer, Sam 34, 64, 66, 71, 72, 83, 92, 96, 102, 111
Fray Marcos de Niza 11
Fruitland Cemetery 16

G

Gardner, Charlie 108
Gardner, Hettie Lee 37, 88
Gardner, Virginia 108
Gatlin, Leota 91
Geiger, Mr. 108
German Baptist 10, 41
Goldwater, Barry 113
Greene Cattle Company 101
Grennan, Judy 82
Grennan, Nancy 82
Grennan, Sally 82, 86

H

Hanson, V.P. 14
Hawks, Howard 75
Hedgcock, Joan 86
Helvetia Mines 101
Hill, Faye 88
Holbrook, Jane 82
Homestead Act 21
Homestead Land Grant 54
Honnas, Della 108
Houston, Edna 91
Houston, Nathanial 61
Hutchinson, Buell 78
Hutchinson, Kit 78, 88

I

Immigration Service Agents 38
Isaacs, Hank 103

J

Jolly, Frank 62
Jones, Barbara Bowers 91
Juniata College 16

K

Kansas City Star 32
Kelley, Lynn Fraizer 9, 106, 109, 111
Kino, Father Eusebio Francisco 11
Kunde, Minnie 86

L

Lazy 7 Slash 7 69
LeGendre, Ed 108
Lewiston, PA 40
Lindsey, Byrd 89
Little Outfit Ranch School 78
Los Encinos Guest Ranch 47
Lowy, Kay 86, 102

M

Maier, B. 36
Maier Brothers Store 30, 36

Martin, Donnie 28
Mayor of Elgin 74
McCarty, John 25, 46, 55, 65, 83, 108
McCarty, Rhoda Swigart 4, 12, 13, 15, 17, 20, 26, 29, 30, 34, 36, 38, 41, 43, 45, 46, 48, 51, 52, 56, 65, 66, 83, 108
McPherson, Clyde 38
Mellor, Cassie 86
Mendoza, Joker 108
Mennonites 10, 41
Miami, AZ 52
Mock, Delmar, M.D. 104
Model T Ford 71
Morgan, Monta Carol 14, 37
Moss, Austin 99
Moss, Marka Collie 10, 50, 82, 86, 99
Mount Wrightson 18
Mustang Mountains 48, 77, 94
Mustang Ranch 99

N

Nixon, President Richard 113
Nogales, AZ 13, 17, 37, 38, 66
Nogales Daily Herald 75
Nogales High School 109
Nogales International 88
Nogales Little Theater 81

O

Old Nogales Highway 37

P

Papago Springs 38, 47
Parker, Marilyn 82
Parker, William "Billy" 89
Patagonia, AZ 37, 65, 91, 107
Patagonia High School 70, 108
Patagonia Women's Club 89, 99
Pennsylvania Dutch 40
Pennsylvania Railroad Company 61
Perrill, Sharon Everhart 61
Perrin, Dr. E. B. 13
Philadelphia, PA 16, 17
Pierce School 16

Pima County 53
Pioneer Hall 113
Piper, Bill 95, 99
Piper, Posy 10, 84
Piper, Tom 84
Postmistress at Elgin 61
Post Office at Elgin 32
Presidents Day 83
Putnam, Charles 104, 108
Putnam., Dorothy 108
Putnam, Fred 108

Q

Quakers 10, 41
Quiroga, Joe 10

R

Rail X 36
Rain Valley 53, 55, 84
Rain Valley Schoolhouse 47
Red River 74, 76
Roath, Mrs. 86
Rogos, Cheryl 10, 18, 22, 113
Rogos, Tom 10
Rolla, MO 51, 53
Roosevelt, President Theodore 47
Roosevelt, Quentin 47
Rose Tree Ranch 99
Rothrock, Bruce 12, 15, 17, 22, 25, 30, 38, 44, 46, 48, 55, 58, 65, 108
Rothrock, Esther 12, 15, 22, 30, 41, 42, 44, 45, 46, 48, 55, 65, 108
Rothrock, Marie 46
Rothrock, Oliver 15, 17, 22, 25, 30, 48, 58
Rothrock, Oliver II 108
Rowley, Fred 96
Rowley, Jean Fraizer 70, 71, 76, 83, 86, 91, 96, 104, 111
Rowley, Jim 9, 59, 63, 102, 104, 106, 109, 111, 112

S

Salem, OR 108
San Ignacio del Babacomari 11
San Rafael Valley 38, 78
Santa Cruz County 53
Santa Cruz County Cowbelles 89

Santa Cruz County Fair 99
Santa Cruz County Fair and Rodeo Association 61, 111
Santa Cruz River 13
Schock, Esther 81
Schock, Lou 88
Schorr, Marie 88
Seven Cities of Cibola 11
Sierra Vista, AZ 36
Sims, Deanna 86
Sonoita, AZ 38
Sonoita Crossroads 96
Sonoita/Elgin Fire Association 112
Sonoita Horse Races 88
Sonoita Rodeo 88
Southern Pacific Railroad 30, 60, 107
Southern Pacific station house 28
Speed, Mr. 108
Spencer, Jokie 95, 112
Star Theatre in Nogales 81
State Livestock Board 68
Stoddard, Emory 108
Superintendent of Schools for Santa Cruz County 61
Swigart, Christian Hanawalt 43
Swigart, Elizabeth 40, 42, 44, 46, 47, 48
Swigart, James William 42
Swigart, J.C. 67
Swigart, John Goodman 43
Swigart, Mary Jane 43
Swigart, Samuel James 40, 42, 44, 46, 47, 48, 65, 66, 67
Swinging H Ranch 99

T

Telles, Bill 91
Telles, David 91
Texaco Company 52
Texaco service station 96, 102
Thompson, Janet Rowley 9, 104, 106, 111, 112
Tombstone 48, 65
Tovrea, Harold 99
Tucson, AZ 53
Turney, Ida 84

U

Udall, Morris 113
United States General Land Office Survey stake 22

V

Van Gorder, Gerry 86, 87
Van Gorder, Russell 87
Vaughn Church 108
Villa, Pancho 38, 47

W

Washington's Birthday 82
Wayne, John 74, 78
West Gate to Fort Huachuca 61
White, Donna 82
White, Gladys 82
White, John 108
Williams, Jack 113
Williams, Jane 88
Wilson, C. B. "Chris" 37
Wilson, Dyke 53
Wilson, President Woodrow 54
Wilson, Sarah 53
Winterhaven subdivision 109

Y

Yeary, Earl 25
Yeary, Gus 25

Betty Barr

Arizona Cattlewoman

About the Author

(Bob Kimball photo)

Betty Barr is an award-winning author and journalist, who specializes in uncovering hidden treasures – the people places and things unique to southeastern Arizona. Her previous books include *Hidden Treasures of Santa Cruz County, More Hidden Treasures of Santa Cruz County, A John Slaughter Kid, the Story of May Watkins Burns,* and *Around Sonoita,* one of the Images of America series by Arcadia Publishing.

She co-edited, with Dr. William J. Kelly, a revised edition of *Arizona in the '50s,* a firsthand account of frontier life in 1857 by Capt. James Tevis.

Her work has appeared in numerous publications including Arizona Highways, Arabian Horse, Range Magazine and Arizona Quarter Horse News. She was a regular contributor to the *Nogales International* and *Weekly Bulletin* newspapers for 20 years.

In 2009, Betty co-chaired a project to construct the Bowman and Stradling History Center at the Fairgrounds in Sonoita, which contains numerous western and ranching artifacts of the area. Included are selected displays from the original Anne Stradling Museum of the Horse in Patagonia, and an impressive collection of oral histories and photographs collected by the late Bob Bowman, a local historian.

In 2014 she chaired an all-day celebration in conjunction with the Smithsonian Institution's traveling exhibit entitled Journey Stories, held at the Bowman and Stradling History Center. Over 400 people attended the event which explored westward and northward migration to the area.

Her chronicles of the history of the legendary Empire Ranch south of Tucson were adapted as a promotional piece by the Bureau of Land Management and the Empire Ranch Foundation. It was used as a historical handout at the annual Empire Ranch Roundup and Western Art show in 2004.

A graduate of the University of Arizona, she lives in Sonoita, Arizona with her husband John.

CPSIA information can be obtained
at www.ICGtesting.com
Printed in the USA
FSOW02n1749130817
37419FS